Sinbad The Sa

A Pantomime

John Morley

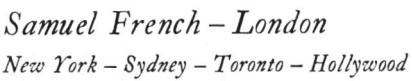

© 1983 BY JOHN MORLEY

Rights of Performance by Amateurs are controlled by Samuel French Ltd, 52 Fitzroy Street, London W1P 6JR, and they, or their authorized agents, issue licences to amateurs on payment of a fee. **It is an infringement of the Copyright to give any performance or public reading of the play before the fee has been paid and the licence issued.**

The Royalty Fee indicated below is subject to contract and subject to variation at the sole discretion of Samuel French Ltd.

Basic fee for each and every
performance by amateurs   Code L
in the British Isles

The publication of this play does not imply that it is necessarily available for performance by amateurs or professionals, either in the British Isles or Overseas. Amateurs and professionals considering a production are strongly advised in their own interests to apply to the appropriate agents for consent before starting rehearsals or booking a theatre or hall.

ISBN 0 573 16441 X

Please see page iv for further copyright information.

CHARACTERS

Sinbad the Sailor, the ship's captain
Mrs Semolina Sinbad, the ship's cook and Sinbad's mother
Tinbad the Tailor, the sailmaker and Mrs Sinbad's friend
Mustapha Kit-Kat, the ship's bosun
The Caliph of Constantinople
The Princess Pearl, his bride-to-be
Sinistro, the wicked sorcerer
Talida, a native girl of Nirvana
Crunchbones, the witchdoctor of Nirvana
The Old Man of the Sea
Bludruncolda, the evil priestess at the Shrine of Love
El Hump, a disdainful camel
The Man-Eating Plant
The Wazir of Constantinople
Coca
Cola } Ex-members of the Caliph's harem
Scrubdeck, the cabin boy
Mazola, the galley girl

Chorus:
Playing Citizens of Constantinople; natives of Nirvana; living statues of the Grotto; exotic birds or jungle animals; slaves at the Shrine of Love; guests at Sinbad's wedding

COPYRIGHT INFORMATION

(See also page ii)

This play is fully protected under the Copyright Laws of the British Commonwealth of Nations, the United States of America and all countries of the Berne and Universal Copyright Conventions.

All rights, including Stage, Motion Picture, Radio, Television, Public Reading, and Translation into Foreign Languages, are strictly reserved.

No part of this publication may lawfully be reproduced in ANY form or by any means—photocopying, typescript, recording (including video-recording), manuscript, electronic, mechanical, or otherwise—or be transmitted or stored in a retrieval system, without prior permission.

Licences for amateur performances are issued subject to the understanding that it shall be made clear in all advertising matter that the audience will witness an amateur performance; that the names of the authors of the plays shall be included on all announcements and on all programmes; and that the integrity of the authors' work will be preserved.

The Royalty Fee is subject to contract and subject to variation at the sole discretion of Samuel French Ltd.

In Theatres or Halls seating Four Hundred or more the fee will be subject to negotiation.

In Territories Overseas the fee quoted in this Acting Edition may not apply. A fee will be quoted on application to our local authorized agent, or if there is no such agent, on application to Samuel French Ltd, London.

VIDEO RECORDING OF AMATEUR PRODUCTIONS

Please note that the copyright laws governing video-recording are extremely complex and that it should not be assumed that any play may be video-recorded *for whatever purpose* without first obtaining the permission of the appropriate agents. The fact that a play is published by Samuel French Ltd does not indicate that video rights are available or that Samuel French Ltd controls such rights.

DESCRIPTION OF CHARACTERS

Sinbad is the swashbuckling hero and is a romantic, enthusiastic even cocky sailor from the Middle East. The part can be played by a male or (preferably) a female.

Mrs Sinbad is adventurous, game for anything and — in a daft sort of way — is man-mad. She loves her son but it not too sentimental about it. A part for a man or woman.

Tinbad the Tailor is a warmhearted idiot. As he is Mrs Sinbad's great friend they are almost a "double act". His catchphrase — Kismet — is often used in the stories of the Arabian Nights and it is probable that Nelson didn't say "Kiss me Hardy" but "Kismet Hardy"! Usually male; but sometimes played as a cheeky second principal boy, and female.

The Caliph is dignified, clearly the undisputed ruler of Turkey. He has "presence" in the Arabian Nights tradition.

The Princess Pearl has oriental dignity, in contrast to the more tomboy Talida, and is beautiful. Her scenes are a mixture of defiance, that hides her fear, and a certain dry comedy.

Talida is the principal girl. She is as adventurous as Sinbad and her attractions are tomboyish. She is warm and fun and not dignified.

Sinistro is sinister and scheming. A Spanish Grandee beard helps the "sorcerer" look. Though a smooth and sophisticated villain, he enjoys the audience participation and his every exit is stylized.

Crunchbones is the witchdoctor who would like to have Sinistro's style but with his voice and costume he is almost comical, though terrifying at times.

The Old Man of the Sea is a cruelly eccentric old villain, but we discover he is vulnerable. Hs is usually played by a female for he is so old that his voice should be thin, high-pitched and witch-like. Male, or (preferably) female.

Bludruncolda is a female Sinistro. She can be played as a hardened young girl or middle-aged. There is something of the wicked Queen in *Snow White* about her.

Mustapha Kit-Kat is a friendly nit-wit, the crony of Tinbad, and can be played by a girl as a cheeky comedy "second principal boy". Male or female.

The Wazir is a middle-aged dignified man, or he can be a bustling Oriental Sergeant Major.

El Hump the disdainful camel. If he turns his head away when asked a question he seems very disdainful indeed. He dances a softshoe. Preferably two females.

Coca and **Cola** are attractive and somewhat dizzy slave girls.

ACT I

SCENE 1   The Quayside at Constantinople where the Caliph's honeymoon ship is moored
SCENE 2   Aboard Sinbad's ship on the high seas
SCENE 3   The dreaded Sacrifice Stone on the Island of Nirvana
SCENE 4   Outside the Grotto of the Old Man of the Sea
SCENE 5   (A) Inside the Grotto of Living Statues
           (B) The Gates to the Emerald Valley

ACT II

SCENE 1   The Nest of the Giant Roc Bird in the Emerald Valley
SCENE 2   The Jungle of Man-Eating Plants near the Shrine
SCENE 3   The Shrine of Love and the Waters of Eternal Happiness
SCENE 4   Aboard Sinbad's ship returning home
SCENE 5   Sinbad's wedding in the Palace of a Million Minarets in Constantinople

This pantomime is often presented spectacularly but if a small production is required, a Permanent Set style can easily be used. See scenery notes at the end of the play.

MUSIC SUGGESTIONS

The songs suggested are based on audience research, for pantomime audiences like to hear the songs they know. They like "standards". You are, of course, welcome to alter the choice of songs but please remember that a licence issued by Samuel French Ltd to perform the pantomime does not include permission to use copyright songs and music. Please read the notice supplied by the Performing Right Society, which follows this list of Music Suggestions.

The publishers of the suggested music are given in brackets after the song title.

Overture   Main songs, linked with Arabian Nights style music (Theme Music)

Song

1 The Fleet's In Port Again (Noel Gay Ltd) — **Turkish Citizens**
2 Rolling (Sailing?) Round the World (Sun Music) — **Sinbad** and **Citizens**
3 All the Nice Girls Love a Sailor (EMI Music) — **Mrs Sinbad** and **Citizens**
   Reprise of Song 1 — **Company** except **Princess** and **Sinistro**
4 Now the Boat Is All Afloat (almost *Knees Up, Mother Brown*) — **Sinbad, Mrs Sinbad, Tinbad, Mustapha** (and two others?)
5 Kim-Ba-Ay (F. & R. Walsh Ltd) *or* Sabre Dance (F. & R. Walsh Ltd) and Dem Bones, Dem Dry Bones (Foyles Music Dept) — **Witchdoctor** and **Islanders**
6 Around the World I've Searched For You (Chappell) — **Sinbad** and **Talida**
7 You're The One That I Want (Chappell) — **Mrs Sinbad** and **Islanders**
8 Only You (And You Alone) (Chappell) *or* Who Can I Turn To? (Conrad Music) — **Princess** and offstage **Islanders**
9 Thank U Very Much (Noel Gay Ltd) — **Old Man of the Sea, Sinbad, Talida, Mrs Sinbad, Mustapha**
10 Ballin' The Jack (EMI Music) *or* — **Living Statues**

	Let The Sun Shine In (United Artists) Reprise of Song 6	All, except **Sinistro** and **Princess**
	INTERVAL	
11	Hey Little Hen (Noel Gay Ltd) *or* Chick, Chick, Chicken (Campbell Connolly) *and* Rock Around the Clock (Kassner Music)	**Birds** **Birds** and **Islanders**
12	Sheik of Araby (Feldman Music)	**Mrs Sinbad, Tinbad** and **Camel**
13	Get A Little Sand Between Your Toes (Macauley Music) *or* Oh, Island in the Sun (Chappell)	**Talida** and two juvenile **Islanders**
14	*Music*: Ride of the Valkyries — Wagner	**Roc Bird**'s Arrival
15	Parody of *Jingle Bells*	
16	Hawaiian Wedding Song (F. & R. Walsh Ltd) *or* Fantasy Island (Music Sales Ltd)	**Slaves of the Shrine** and **Priestess**
17	Dance, In The Old Fashioned Way (Chappell)	**Mrs Sinbad, Tinbad** and **Slaves**
	Reprise of Song 6	**Company**
18	Yellow Submarine (Northern Songs)	**Mrs Sinbad, Tinbad** and **Audience**
	Reprise of Song 3 (For Finale Walkdown)	**Company**

If you have any difficulty in obtaining sheet music the National Operatic and Dramatic Association, NODA House, 1 Crestfield Street, London, WC1H 8AU would be pleased to help.

The following statement concerning the use of music is printed here on behalf of the Performing Right Society Ltd, by whom it was supplied

The permission of the owner of the performing right in copyright music must be obtained before any public performance may be given, whether in conjunction with a play or sketch or otherwise, and this permission is just as necessary for amateur performances as for professional. The majority of copyright musical works (other than oratorios, musical plays and similar dramatico–musical works) are controlled in the British Commonwealth by the PERFORMING RIGHT SOCIETY LTD, 29–33 BERNERS STREET, LONDON W1P 4AA.

The Society's practice is to issue licences authorizing the use of its repertoire to the proprietors of premises at which music is publicly performed, or, alternatively, to the organizers of musical entertainments, but the Society does not require payment of fees by performers as such. Producers or promoters of plays, sketches, etc., at which music is to be performed, during or after the play or sketch, should ascertain whether the premises at which their performances are to be given are covered by a licence issued by the Society, and if they are not, should make application to the Society for particulars as to the fee payable.

ACT I

Scene 1

The Quayside at Constantinople. (See note on settings at the end of the play)

As the Curtain *rises the Theme Music, with Arabian percussion effects, is heard. A Beggar squats at one side, playing a flute, with a basket beside him. A snake rises from the basket*

On the opposite side of the stage the Wazir stands salaaming to the Audience, with the slave girls Coca and Cola kneeling on the floor, one each side of him, salaaming and calling out loudly

Wazir
Coca } (*together, over the percussion effects*)   Salaam! Salaam!
Cola

Wazir (*to the Audience*)   Greetings, good people! I am the Grand Wazir of the Caliph and I welcome you to Constantinople!
Coca   It is here in this great capital that the most famous of all Eastern stories is about to begin!
Cola   Come then to this city of slave markets, of oriental bazaars, of magic and mystery!

The Arabian style percussion continues quietly under the Wazir's prologue

Wazir   Many moons ago, in the Ancient City of Constantinople, there lived a beautiful Princess! She was loved by all the people and she was also loved by the great Caliph. But alas, she was *also* loved by a wicked sorcerer called Sinistro.

There is a dramatic chord

How she was rescued from this evil man by our hero Sinbad the Sailor, is a story from the wondrous book of the Arabian Nights! Good people, it is a beautiful day — a day in the romantic city of Constantinople — it is the day when Sinbad and his crew are returning home and even now his ship has reached the quayside!

There is a crash from percussion and Turkish Citizens run on to form a group round the Wazir

The Company, including the snake charmer, sing:

Song 1

There is a short dance routine and then all line the footlights, clapping in time and encouraging the Audience to clap as they sing the chorus

After the song the Wazir exits

1st Citizen (*pointing offstage*) Look, Tinbad's arrived!
2nd Citizen Here he is, Tinbad the Tailor!

Tinbad runs in

Tinbad (*to everyone*) Hallo, Cassim! Hallo, Hassan! Hallo, Sandra—Shalimar—Zelda!
All (*in turn*) Hallo, Tinbad!
Tinbad Where's the Wazir?
All Why?
Tinbad Well he wazir a moment ago! Oh it's good to be home after another voyage! (*He stamps his feet*) It's nice to have your feet on terra cotta. How are you, Citizens?
All Fine!
Tinbad (*seeing the Audience*) Oh look, *more* citizens! (*Waving to the Audience*) Gunaydin! Marhaba! Gunaydin! Marhaba! That's Turkish for "good morning" in case you think I've gone mad. How are you? All right?

The Audience is encouraged to reply

But we haven't been properly introduced! I'm Tinbad the Tailor—I make the sails for Sinbad's ship. It's a hard job—especially in the winter. Have you ever tried to make the January sails?
Young Girl Yes—at Lewis's! (*Or local store*)
Tinbad (*to her*) Hallo sunshine. I've just come back from sailing the Seven Seas with Sinbad. D'you know which are the Seven Seas?

The Young Girl shakes her head. So Tinbad asks the others

All right, *you* tell me the Seven Seas.
1st Citizen (*calling*) The Red Sea—
2nd Citizen The Dead Sea—
3rd Citizen The North Sea—
4th Citizen The Black Sea—
5th Citizen The Irish Sea—
6th Citizen The China Sea—
Tinbad Well come on, you can't stop there, there's one more sea!
Young Girl Suck it and see!

Everyone laughs

Tinbad (*to the Young Girl*) Listen cheeky, if you don't shut up I'll be disturbin' your turban. (*To the Audience*) Now you must meet the two slave girls. (*To Coca*) Tell them who you are, oh Angel Delight.
Coca I'm Coca. (*She gives an Arabian bow to the Audience*)
Cola And I'm Cola. (*She gives an Arabian bow to the Audience*)
Tinbad (*to the Audience*) They're part of the Caliph's harem.

> "My name is Abdul Ben Barum
> I've got sixty-five wives in my harem
> If you're sitting at home

Act I, Scene 1

>And you're sick of your own
>Take a couple of mine—I can spare 'em!"

Everyone laughs

>How did you manage to meet the Caliph in the first place?
>
>**Coca** He came to our village to find a little peace—and I was the little piece.

Cola sways about seductively, belly dancer/slave girl style, to Arabian percussion while the Citizens wolf whistle

>How d'you like my slave girl costume?
>
>**Tinbad** If I say something rude about it I hope you'll laugh it off!

Cola stops swaying

>**Cola** What? Coca, you'd better tell him the latest news.
>**Coca** The Caliph is getting married so we shall have to leave the harem.
>**Tinbad** (*surprised*) Leave the harem?
>**Cola** We're moving to a rich man named Abdul Aziz.
>**Tinbad** It's not fair! Why can't I have a couple of slave girls if Abdul Aziz?

Everyone laughs

>**Tinbad** (*to the Audience*) Oh it's good to laugh after all the frights I've had on my travels. But I've an Eastern way of putting things right when I'm frightened. (*To Coca and Cola*) Bring on the motto!

The two girls exit

>When we're in a tight spot all we have to do is remember it's Fate. If a gale blows and we think we might get shipwrecked, we don't worry, we just say the word!

Coca and Cola return, stand close together and hold up two boards. The first says "MET" and the other says "KIS"

>So here I am on the deck of Sinbad's ship, really frightened but this is where you help me. Just call out the word on the board! (*Without looking, he points to the board*) Come on, altogether!
>
>**Citizens** and **Audience** MET ... KIS!
>
>**Tinbad** What? What you talking about. "Metkiss"? (*He looks at the girls*) You sloppy slave girls—wrong way round—change places!

The girls change places

>That's better. (*To the Audience, acting it out*) I'm climbing up the rigging and I'm frightened but you call out ... (*he points to the boards*)
>
>**Citizens** and **Audience** KISMET!
>**Tinbad** I can't hear you. I've got all this dirty washing on my head. (*He acts it out again*) I'm frightened! I'm frightened!
>**Citizens** and **Audience** KISMET!
>**Tinbad** (*with a big smile, giving the "thumbs-up" sign*) Thanks—I'm better now! Once again ... (*acting it out*) ... I'm frightened, I'm frightened!
>**Citizens** and **Audience** KISMET!

Tinbad Thanks—I'm better now! See you later!

Tinbad exits, waving, L

1st Citizen (*pointing* R) From Lisbon to Liberia—
2nd Citizen (*pointing*) From Aden to Algeria—
3rd Citizen (*pointing*) From Athens to Australia—
4th Citizen (*pointing*) Here comes Sinbad the Sailor!

Up tempo music starts and Sinbad strides in, waving to the Citizens

Sinbad Greetings!
Citizens Greetings, Sinbad!
Sinbad (*shaking hands boisterously*) Great to be home! Hullo! Nice to see you ... to see you ...
Citizens Nice!
Sinbad Well, here I am back home in Constantinople but I still haven't found me a wife ...
All Aaaaah ...
Sinbad Thanks for your concern. I've been on *six* voyages and I still haven't found the girl for me. Ah well, I've enjoyed sailing round the world—it's been great!

Sinbad sings

Song 2

Soon the Citizens join Sinbad and the song becomes a

PRODUCTION NUMBER

After the number all exit except Sinbad who waves goodbye, moving upstage

The lights darken, there is dramatic music and Sinistro, carrying a large book, enters DL

Sinistro (*triumphantly*) Ha, ha, ha! At last, by my magic power I've reached Constantinople! Now to find out about the beautiful Princess Pearl, for it is she that makes my heart beat like the hammers of Hydrabad!
(*Reciting, and pacing along footlights*)

> I'm Sinistro the Sorcerer
> I'm wicked and I'm vile
> But when I work my wickedness
> I do the thing in style
> I'm elegantly evil
> I'm the tops of my profession
> But I've come to Constantinople
> Because of an obsession
> With love I'm overladen
> And that's the honest truth
> Who can take me to this maiden?
> Ah look—a puny youth!

Act I, Scene 1   5

(*Calling to Sinbad*) My boy! Perhaps you can help me?
Sinbad You look lost, you must be a stranger.
Sinistro I come from over the sea, from the island of Nirvana. And you?
Sinbad I'm Sinbad the Sailor, I've just come home to Constantinople.
Sinistro And what do you think of the Wonder of the Orient?
Sinbad The wonder of the Orient? Well they're top of the league, aren't they?
Sinistro I mean, what do you think of your beautiful Princess? (*With great emphasis*) And when is she due to leave the palace?
Sinbad Who are you that you want to know?
Sinistro (*impressively*) I'm Sinistro.
Sinbad (*sympathizing*) You don't look too well.
Sinistro No, no, Sinistro's my name. I am a sorcerer.
Sinbad Did you arrive on a magic carpet? Are you a flying sorcerer?

Sinbad laughs but Sinistro turns on him in a rage

Sinistro SILENCE!
Sinbad All right, all right, keep your hair on!
Sinistro I am Sinistro the Sorcerer. I am all powerful. I am a conjuror.
Sinbad (*with Tommy Cooper-style gesture*) Just like that! So tell me about your magic.
Sinistro I will. (*Fitting actions to his words*) Not long ago I met a beautiful girl in Baghdad and having hypnotized her, I levitated her. (*He gazes upwards*)
Sinbad You mean, she went up in the air? (*He gazes upwards*) It must have looked incredible!
Sinistro It did. (*Romantically*) I'll never forget seeing Dawn rising over the rooftops of Baghdad ...
Sinbad (*laughing*) And was that the end of your magic?
Sinistro Certainly not. For an encore I waved my arms at the nearby Mosque and set it on fire.
Sinbad Set the Mosque on fire? Holy smoke! Then let me have a look at your magic book!
Sinistro No, no! (*He holds it closer*)
Sinbad Yes, yes! Why not? Is it full of magic spells? (*He grabs the book*) I'm interested in magic, and perhaps ... (*He opens the book and is astonished*) Why, it's full of pictures of the Princess!
Sinistro (*to the Audience*) Curses! He's found out my secret! (*Recovering and bluffing*) I'm merely an admirer of hers. I'm a Royalist, I read the *Daily Telegraph* and *Woman's Weekly*. (*He takes the book back*) I want to see the Princess.
Sinbad Mmmmmmm ... (*to the Audience*) I don't like him, do you?
Audience No!
Sinbad D'you think I can trust him?
Audience No!
Sinbad (*looking at Sinistro*) Oh he's harmless ... *I think*. You're a harmless man so I'll tell you; the Princess that you fancy so much is due here very soon. In fact, she is to marry the Caliph of Constantinople this very day!

There is a dramatic chord

Sinistro (*aghast*) The Caliph is to marry her?
Sinbad (*nodding*) She's got hazel eyes, chestnut hair, an almond skin — he's nuts about her.
Sinistro (*aside to the Audience*) Marry the Caliph? *This must not happen* ...
Sinbad Yes, isn't it fabulous? They're going to get married and then sail away on the Caliph's honeymoon ship! (*He points to it*)
Sinistro That they must never do. (*To the Audience*) This boy will be useful — I must be nice to him. (*To Sinbad*) Would you like to see the girl you will one day marry?
Sinbad Ach — you're pulling my leg!
Sinistro Silence, boy ... and watch carefully. I can call on the spirits of Nirvana ...

Sinistro waves his arms about creating a spell. The Lights fade down and mysterious music is heard as he intones and waves his arms towards the ship

    (*Chanting*)   Abracadabra and the light goes dim,
                          Show the girl of his dreams to him!

Upstage, in the half light, a Hawaiian style girl — Talida — is seen behind the gauze panel of the Caliph's ship

Sinbad (*delighted*) A million thanks! For that girl seems
                      To be the girl I've met in my dreams!
                      I've never seen such a beautiful sight —
                      Oh you're a fabulous sorcerer, all right!

He looks upstage again but the lights have dimmed and Talida has gone

Sinbad She's vanished!
Sinistro You are pleased with her, oh boy they call Sinbad the Sailor?
Sinbad Pleased? I'm so happy I'll do exactly what you want! I'll bring you back here the moment the Princess arrives!
Sinistro (*rubbing his hands together*) Good boy, you're a little treasure. (*To himself, laughing evilly*) Everything's working out *beautifully*! (*This becomes his "catchphrase"*)
Sinbad Meanwhile, I'll let you meet my Mum! I'd better find her or she'll have me on the carpet. (*Calling*) Mum! Where are you! Mrs Sinbad! Mum!

Sinbad exits

Sinistro Yes, everything's working out *beautifully*. (*He laughs evilly*) Ha, ha, ha!

Sinistro follows Sinbad off

The bouncy introduction to Song 3 is heard and Mrs Sinbad enters with a big coloured bag

Mrs Sinbad Hullo everybody! And is everybody happy?

The Audience are encouraged to reply

    Goody gum drops! Well, *I'm* Sinbad's Mum. Yes, I'm Mrs Semolina

Act I, Scene 1

Sinbad. (*To someone in the Audience*) No, dear, not Argentina, Semolina. Semolina Sinbad. I wasn't always called Mrs Sinbad. I've got through three husbands and Mr Sinbad was the last. Poor man, he was killed by a number eighteen bus. He died of exposure — waiting for it. So now I'm looking for another husband. Oh I may have been over the hurdles three times but I'm still game for the National! (*She peers at the Audience*) I wonder if one of you might do. Ah, there's somebody in the second row — just my type — I like my men in big hunks! (*Peering again*) Oh and he's bald so he looks perfect! As for me, I must look a perfect sight!

She takes a plastic toilet seat and lid from her large bag and uses it like a compact

I *do* look a sight, I thought I did. Well, no wonder! I was walking down the gangplank of Sinbad's ship and this speed boat comes whizzing into the harbour — and nearly hurled me into Maternity! Look at my dress! And my shoes!

She bends down to look at them and a large prop fish that appeared to be part of her hat decoration falls onto the ground

A kipper off my titfer! Oh, isn't that the twelve mile limit!

She throws the fish into the wings and a large splash is heard

And getting wet like this has brought on this pain again. I went to the Doctor and asked him what it was and he says I've got a touch of flexible rostering. It's all down my front here and down my back here —

She turns round and there is a big crab or lobster attached to her seat

The pain's quite nippy. Still, when we get back from a voyage I always stay at that nice house over there with my friend, Tinbad the Tailor. He's only got a small room at the front but I've got a large flat behind. (*To the Audience*) What d'you mean, you can see I have? I've just been buying some food and you're probably wondering what we eat in Constantinople. I'll give you a clue — listen!

The music of a famous chocolate commercial is heard

Have a guess... What? Kellogg's Corn Flakes? What you mean, Kellogg's Corn Flakes? No, Fry's Turkish Delight! (*Looking at the Audience*) Honestly, some mothers do have 'em! Now, in case you've never tasted Turkish food, would you like a sample? You would? Here you are then!

She throws a few bars of Turkish Delight into the Audience. For the last one she makes a great moment of it by going upstage and then running down and bowling the bar to the back of the Audience, and whirling her arm round and round like a windmill before she throws

I'm the cook on Sinbad's ship and I give the crew chocolate every night. Well, not a big bar like that but just a teeny square of chocolate — I don't know what they're for but they keep the crew going. And Sinbad's crew are lovely boys — and I do like seamen! All us girls in Constantinople like sailors! (*She calls offstage*) Girls, I'm telling them that all us girls like sailors and it's true, isn't it?

The Citizens enter

Citizens (*as they enter*) Yes — of course it is — we all fancy the navy — hullo Mrs Sinbad!

Mrs Sinbad sings

Song 3

Mrs Sinbad dances with the chorus

After the song everyone exits

Sinbad enters

Sinbad (*calling*) Mum! Oh, Mum!

Mrs Sinbad returns, panting heavily after her hectic dance

Mrs Sinbad Oh — oh — I'm just getting me breath back — why did you have to call me back so soon?
Sinbad It's the way we rehearsed this bit.
Mrs Sinbad (*looking at him then at the Audience*) Cheeky devil isn't he? (*To Sinbad*) All right, what is it?
Sinbad You know how poor we are.
Mrs Sinbad Don't I just.
Sinbad Well I think we're going to be rich! I've just met a sorcerer and he's promised me money! All I have to do is point out the Princess when she arrives!
Mrs Sinbad Promises. Promises. We may be poor but I warn you: never speak to strange men.
Sinbad (*groaning*) Oh, Mum.
Mrs Sinbad I did once and a really terrible thing happened to me.
Sinbad What was that?
Mrs Sinbad I married him.

An oriental fanfare sounds

Sinbad That'll be the Princess now — I must go and collect the sorcerer. (*Waving*) Wotcher!
Mrs Sinbad Wotcher? You are common, you're common as muck. (*To the Audience*) Why can't he talk proper — like David Bellamy?

Mrs Sinbad and Sinbad exit

There is a fanfare. Coca and Cola enter in procession followed by the Wazir and the Citizens, prominent among them being Mustapha, who waves like royalty

Coca   Oh Eastern people lend an ear!
Cola   A message from the Grand Wazir!
Wazir   Our great and good Caliph is here!

Act I, Scene 1 9

Coca His heart is warmer than the Sun!
Cola His blessings like the fountains run!

The Wazir is about to speak again but Mustapha interrupts

Mustapha So a happy new year to everyone!

All laugh, except the Wazir

Wazir Silence, you son of a camel driver.
Mustapha I was only trying to ...
Wazir Salaam!
Mustapha I wanted to add a bit of ...
Wazir When I say salaam you will salaam!
Mustapha (*to the Audience*) It's Len Murray.

All except Mustapha start to kneel down and salaam

Wazir All will salaam! Make way for the Ruler of the Seventeen Mountains! His Unutterable Magnificence the Caliph of Constantinople and his Bride to be, the Princess Pearl! Grovel! Grovel!

Mustapha is still standing

Mustapha (*grinning at him*) What?
Wazir Grovel, oh moonface.
Mustapha Oh *grovel*! What you put on the garden path!
Wazir (*with narrowed eyes*) What is your name?
Mustapha Mustapha.
Wazir Mustapha who?
Mustapha No, Mustapha Kit-Kat.
Wazir (*groaning*) Please. Give me a break.
Mustapha Yes, I'm one of Sinbad's crew! I'm the ship's Bosun! I'm important I am! I'm going to ...
Wazir (*thunderously*) You're going to grovel.
Mustapha I'll bow. That'll be enough.

Another fanfare is heard as all bow and salaam. The dignified Caliph enters, followed by a litter or oriental-style sedan chair in which the Princess Pearl is sitting. The curtains or door to it are closed, and it is taken across the stage and put down by the far wings

(*To the Audience*) You'll notice his Majesty has got a white face. That's why they call him the Milk Sheik. Boom! Boom!
Caliph Greetings, my good people!
All (*rising*) Greetings!
Caliph Where are Coca and Cola?
Both Here, oh master.
Caliph Is everything prepared for my honeymoon trip?
Coca We checked with (*local travel agency*)
Caliph Good. Then let her Royal Highness show herself to my people!

At his command, Coca and Cola move to the litter and ceremonially open each curtain or door

Downstage Sinbad runs in with Sinistro

Sinbad (*pointing*) There's the Princess!
Sinistro (*rubbing his hands*) Aha! (*To the Audience*) The moment I've been waiting for!

A few bars of the Theme Music are played as Coca and Cola help the Princess from the litter. The beautiful girl steps out and Sinistro reacts greatly. The Princess smiles at the slave girls then at the Citizens who are calling out

All Salaam, Princess! Salaam! Salaam!
Princess Salaam, my good people! May Allah grant that I will be a good Princess and bring you peace and prosperity!

The Princess and Caliph talk to a group of Citizens

Sinistro The Princess! The answer to my every dream!
(*to the Audience*) Now I must think up some magical scheme...

(*He schemes at the downstage* L *corner*)

Tinbad enters, R, *singing happily. He sees the Caliph and addresses the Audience*

Tinbad (*terrified*) It's the Caliph of Constantinople! I'm frightened, I'm frightened!

The Audience will hopefully shout "Kismet"

(*Giving a "thumbs-up" sign*) Thanks—I'm better now! (*To the Caliph*) Your Magnificence! Your Municipal Car Park!
Wazir Any more insolence from you and you'll be put in the dungeons.
Princess (*to the Wazir and Caliph*) He means no harm. He's just full of natural ebullience and the good things of life.
Tinbad (*to the Audience*) She makes me sound like All Bran!
Princess (*laughing*) You should be our court jester! Who are you?
Tinbad I'm Tinbad the Tailor and (*indicating Sinbad*) this here is my friend, Sinbad the Sailor.
Sinbad Your Grace, we all hope that when you are married you will live happily ever after.
Tinbad Don't call her Your Grace. Call her Sultana—that's her current title.
Caliph My beloved, return to your palanquin and go aboard our honeymoon ship—together we will make it the Boat of Dreams, for it is written that it shall be so, and Destiny never lies.

The Princess is helped into her litter (which must be by the wings). Coca draws the curtains, hiding her. Everyone turns to move towards the litter, and waves

1st Citizen May Allah protect you!
2nd Citizen Blessings on the Princess!
3rd Citizen May Fortune smile on you for ever!

Act I, Scene 1   11

Everyone crowds round the litter, facing upstage, except Sinistro who has remained at the downstage corner

Sinistro   More splendid than diamonds
             More precious than gold!
             In my arms the lovely
             Princess I must hold!
             Spirits of Nirvana come to me here
             AND MAKE THE PRINCESS DISAPPEAR!

Sinistro waves his arms, casting a spell. The stage darkens, dramatic music, thunder crashes out, lightning flashes

Sinistro   I call on the elements! Thunder! Lightning!
             (*shouting*) Weave a magical spell that is frightening!

Everyone turns to Sinistro, clutching each other and frozen in terror. There is silence now

             Listen you fools, to what I'm dreaming of.
             Far across the seas, there is the Shrine of Love.
             Once she has drunk the waters of that Shrine
             Why, then the Princess Pearl forever will be mine!
             (*He waves his arms about, remaining at the downstage corner*)
             Magical spells around me whirl
             Lo and behold—the Princess Pearl!

There is a percussion crash. From the opposite side to the litter, and the people, the Princess enters as though hypnotized

Everyone gasps in horror as Sinistro makes magic passes at her

             The Princess is in my magical sway—
             This has been a highly successful day!

He moves forward, grabs the Princess's wrist with one hand and holds his other on high as he turns to the audience

Everything's working out *beautifully* (*He laughs evilly*) Ha, ha, ha!

There is a crash of thunder, dramatic music and lightning as he drags her across the stage and exits with her, laughing

Everyone becomes "unfrozen" and the Caliph runs forward pointing offstage

Caliph   Come back you villain!

There is a flash in the footlights. The Citizens look at each other in dismay

   (*Scared*) They've both vanished! My beautiful Princess has disappeared!
Sinbad   Your Majesty, he's a sorcerer! I know he's a sorcerer because he spoke to me!
Caliph   He did? Then where is the Shrine of Love? He didn't tell you *that*, did he?

Sinbad Yes he did! He told me his name is Sinistro and he comes from the island of ... of ... (*With horror*) Your Majesty, I can't remember!
Caliph (*enraged*) You can't remember?
Sinbad (*miserably*) No, oh Ruler of the World ... oh Great One, I've forgotten ...
Mustapha You must remember! If you rescue the Princess you'll get the O.B.E.
Sinbad What's that?
Mustapha One Boiled Egg.
Sinbad You're useless—I'll ask Mum. (*Calling*) Mum! Help!

Mrs Sinbad enters

Mrs Sinbad What's the matter, dear? (*She sees the Caliph*) Oh, your Imperial Leather!

Mrs Sinbad curtsies, gets stuck, and Sinbad helps her up

Sinbad What's the name of that place in the South seas—the place with all the palm trees?
Mrs Sinbad Bournemouth?
Sinbad No ... no ...
Mrs Sinbad (*to the Audience*) You're our friends—can *you* remember?

The Audience (or the Musicians) shout out "Nirvana"

Mrs Sinbad Banana?
Sinbad (*to the Audience*) No, no, any of you remember where Evel Knievel comes from?
Audience Nirvana!
Tinbad (*to the Audience*) Yes, I know he's a right nana, but what's the name of the place?
Mustapha (*to the Audience*) Yes, where? ... What? ... What are you talking about?
Caliph (*desperately; to the Audience*) Tell me, I pray you, tell me!
Audience Nirvana.
Sinbad Nirvana! Oh thanks, that's right!
Mrs Sinbad Then tell him, dear, tell him! (*She pushes Sinbad forward*) Go on then, tell Omar Sharif!
Sinbad Your Majesty, the place is called Nirvana!
Caliph (*with relief, calling*) Then come here, Grand Wazir!

The Caliph moves downstage. The Wazir stands beside him, bangs the floor with his stick of office and everyone moves downstage to listen

The CURTAINS *close behind everyone during the following action*

Wazir Pray silence for the Caliph of Constantinople!
Caliph   All Constantinople shall hear this decree:
            I swear as Allah is my rightful Lord
            Whoever brings the Princess back to me
            Then half of my kingdom shall be his reward!

Act I, Scene 2   13

Everyone cheers and Sinbad turns excitedly to his crew

Sinbad   Listen, Mother, Tinbad and all my crew
           Here is what we're going to do
           If half the kingdom is to be the reward
           Now is the time to CLIMB ABOARD!

Everyone sings with Sinbad a short reprise of

Song 1 (reprise)

After the song everyone exits except Mrs Sinbad, Tinbad, Mustapha, Sinbad and Scrubdeck and Mazola, the cabin boy/girl

Either the CURTAINS *remain closed or they open to reveal the front-cloth for Scene 2*

SCENE 2

Aboard Sinbad's ship on the high seas

The action is continuous with the same characters on stage as at the end of Scene 1

Sinbad (*calling upwards through cupped hands*) All aboard! Clear the decks! Batten the hatches! Belay! (*To Mrs Sinbad*) We sail with the tide!
Mrs Sinbad Oh good! I'm all ready, dear! (*She takes a large packet of Tide from her shopping bag*)

   Mrs Sinbad exits

Mustapha Sinbad, can I be the Bos'n?
Sinbad You—the Bos'n?
Mustapha I know all about the navy!
Sinbad Well prove it. Go on, show me you're naval!
Mustapha (*lifting up his shirt*) There!
Sinbad (*shouting upwards*) Hove to! Hove to!
Tinbad (*calling upwards*) Manchester United (*or local football team*) six!
Sinbad Bolster your barnacles!
Tinbad What me? I'll do myself an injury!
Mustapha (*looking offstage; pointing*) Well, shiver me timbers!

Mrs Sinbad marches on L *holding the end of a clothes line on which is suspended a great deal of laundry (bras, long johns, etc.). The stage management hold the rest of the line in the wings*

Mrs Sinbad runs across the stage with the line

Tinbad Is that the laundry line?
Mrs Sinbad No, it's the Onedin Line!

Mrs Sinbad exits R, *giving the stage management her end of the line in the wings* R. *She then runs round the back of the stage, ready to re-enter* L

Meanwhile Sinbad and his crew hold the line up high and pass it along the stage while singing a snatch of sea shanty

Mrs Sinbad now enters L *holding the end of the line (given to her by the stage management)*

Mrs Sinbad (*to the Audience*) They always give you the same old line ...
Sinbad Where's the Mate?
Tinbad At the butchers.
Sinbad No, no, where's the *Mate*?
Tinbad He's around aft.
Mrs Sinbad I know he has, but where is he?
Sinbad He's got the capstan.
Mustapha What a shame, I like Players myself, mind you, what a price cigarettes are ...

Mrs Sinbad bends down to straighten her stocking

Sinbad (*through cupped hands*) Avast behind!
Mrs Sinbad (*clutching her seat*) How dare you!
Sinbad Has everyone got aboard?

Tinbad picks up a piece of plank

Tinbad I've got one! I've got a board!
Mustapha (*heavy Long John Silver style, to Tinbad*) Ar, and if eee makes it all shipshape and Bristol fashion, know what I'll give 'eeee?
Tinbad A bar of old Jamaiccy!
Sinbad Right! There's an important job to do while we sail across the sea to Nirvana. Everybody line up!

The crew lines up. Sinbad paces to and fro in front of them

Sinbad Now this job needs doing really well—right mateys?
All Right!
Sinbad Someone's got to swill out the bilges, empty the garbage, clean all the pumps and loosen the sludge! Whoever wants this job, take one pace forward.

All step one pace back except Mrs Sinbad

Mrs Sinbad Help!

They all laugh. Vaudeville vamp music begins and all sing "Da da da da" and into the following visual routine

Song 4

The tune is almost "Knees Up Mother Brown"

Sinbad   Now the boat is all afloat
　　　　　　 The Captain I shall be

Act I, Scene 2

                        As a member of the crew
                        Here is what I'll do:

Sinbad's gesture is a salute that hits Mrs Sinbad each time his arm comes up, and she reacts furiously

                        Pipe aboard! Pipe aboard!
                        And salute the flag!
                        Pipe aboard! Pipe aboard!
                        And salute the flag!

Mrs Sinbad   Now the boat is all afloat
                        The ship's cook I shall be
                        As a member of the crew
                        Here is what I'll do:

Mrs Sinbad's gestures are stirring then chopping — thus hitting Tinbad with her chop movements, and he reacts with fury

                        Stir the saucepan! Stir the saucepan!
                        And chop up the mince
                        Stir the saucepan! Stir the saucepan!
                        And chop up the mince.

Tinbad   Now the boat is all afloat
                        The sailmaker I'll be
                        As a member of the crew
                        Here is what I'll do:

Tinbad mimes putting huge stitches in a sail, thus hitting Mustapha downwards on the head. He then bends knees low as though doing a sailor's hornpipe movement

                        Stitch in time! Stitch in Time!
                        Hoorah for the rolling sea
                        Stitch in Time! Stitch in Time!
                        Hoorah for the rolling sea.

Mustapha   Now the boat is all afloat
                        The Bosun I will be
                        As a member of the crew
                        Here is what I'll do:

Mustapha makes cleaning gestures as though along the length of the cannon and his gesture hits Tinbad who is also being hit by Mrs Sinbad — in her turn she gets hit by Sinbad and Tinbad

                        Clean the cannon, clean the cannon
                        Push the damper in
                        Clean the cannon, clean the cannon
                        Push the damper in.

The final chorus of everyone singing their own verse is sung very fast, then they all march off, still doing the actions

Optional

Should Scrubdeck the cabin boy and Mazola, the galley girl, join with the others for the routine their verses and actions are as follows

Cabin Boy Now the boat is all afloat
The Cabin Boy I'll be
As a member of the crew
Here is what I'll do:

He puts his hands to his eyes to scan the ocean on "Land ahoy" and as his hand comes up it hits his neighbour. He stamps his foot on the floor — and his other neighbour's foot — on "Drop the anchor down"

Land ahoy! Land ahoy!
Drop the anchor down
Land ahoy! Land ahoy!
Drop the anchor down.

Galley Girl Now the boat is all afloat
The Galley Girl I'll be
As a member of the crew
Here is what I'll do:

She mimes pushing open the porthole window, and then takes the duster tucked in her belt and shakes it in the face of her neighbour in the line-up

Push the porthole, push the porthole
Shake the duster out
Push the porthole, push the porthole
Shake the duster out.

There is a Black-out

In the Black-out loud drum beats and wild cannibal cries are heard. The tabs open or the front-cloth is flown to reveal:

Scene 3

The dreaded Sacrifice Stone on the Island of Nirvana

Weird lighting throws the shadows of the Dancers on to the scenery, maybe Strobe lighting is used. The Hawaiian-style Natives watch the Dancers

Song 5(A)

The dance is in praise of the idol statue, and ends with a howl. The drumbeats continue

  Crunchbones, the Witchdoctor, enters. He carries a pile of big bones

Act I, Scene 3   17

All (*terrified*) Witchdoctor!

As Crunchbones speaks so two Natives drag on the struggling island girl, Talida — the girl Sinbad has seen in his vision in Scene 1

Crunchbones bows to the idol

Crunchbones (*shouting above the drumbeats*) Oh great god of da sea, hear us! We offer you dis sacrifice at da time of da full moon! All dat has been ordered by you shall be done, oh great Bowango, god of da seven seas!

The Natives tie Talida to the stone idol while the Dancers sway and shuffle to and fro

Now Ah must confab with ma bones!

He lays the bones on the floor and he sings

Song 5(B)

During the song the Natives join in the singing and clap in time, becoming more wild and enthusiastic, working the song into a production number

The song ends with the bones ceremonially piled centre stage

Crunchbones (*pointing to the stone idol*) Behold! Dere is da water mark! When da god of da sea brings in da tide, den da waters of Bowango will rise to da watermark, and you shall perish! Boombah!
Talida (*terrified*) No! What crime have I done to deserve this?
Crunchbones You are da most beautiful girl on da island of Nirvana, *dat* is your crime.
Talida (*gasping*) You're mad!
Crunchbones Da god of da sea must be appeased! (*To everyone*) Come!

Still the drum beats continue as Crunchbones collects his bones and exits

All Bawango, god of the sea, we salute you! (*Shouting and waving their spears*) Bawango!

All exit in a stylized shuffling way leaving only Talida on stage

Talida (*sobbing*) I am lost, I am left here to die. Soon the tide will swirl in from the sea and I shall be no more! (*She sobs, and her head droops in despair*)

Downstage Sinbad enters with his scimitar at the ready, and walks across the stage, gazing out front anxiously

Sinbad The island of Nirvana! Now to find the Shrine of Love! Now to rescue the Princess from the wicked sorcerer!
Talida Save me!
Sinbad By the beard of the prophet! (*He runs to Talida*) Save you? Of course I'll save you! Who tied you up like this? (*He undoes the ropes*)
Talida The Witchdoctor. At each full moon there is a sacrifice to the god of the sea.
Sinbad And you're the sacrifice? How horrible! There — you're free.

Talida You have saved me. (*She rubs her wrists*) You are very kind.
Sinbad Nonsense! I'm just a sailor who likes to see a bit of justice being done!
Talida What's your name?
Sinbad Sinbad. What's yours?
Talida Talida.
Sinbad (*romantically*) Talida... what a beautiful name. What other names are people called in Nirvana?
Talida Crunchbones.
Sinbad (*romantically*) Crunchbones... (*Realizing*) Crunchbones?
Talida He's the Witchdoctor.
Sinbad (*laughing*) Crunchbones? You mean he actually *crunches bones*?
Talida Yes.
Sinbad (*seriously*) He *does*? Then what am I laughing at?
Talida Nirvana is not a place for laughter.
Sinbad You're telling me!
Talida It is a place that is in the power of the Witchdoctor!
Sinbad I'll *break* his power! (*Romantically*) And I've a good reason — I've met you before.
Talida But where?
Sinbad In my dreams, and in a vision. So we'll defeat the Witchdoctor — you'll see!
Talida There is also his friend, the Priestess in The Shrine of Love.
Sinbad The Shrine of Love! That's what I've come here to find!
Talida Alas, it is hard to find and the journey is full of danger!
Sinbad I don't care! You see, I've promised the Caliph of Constantinople that I'll bring back his bride, the Princess Pearl!
Talida He loves her very much?
Sinbad It was love at first sight — and that's something I didn't believe could happen. (*He takes her hand*) Even though I've sailed all round the world.
Talida (*smiling*) I will help you. You are a stranger in Nirvana.
Sinbad I'm not only a stranger in Nirvana, I'm a stranger in Paradise.

Song 6

After the short duet they exit hand in hand

The other side, Crunchbones enters with his pile of bones

Crunchbones Soon da tide will be rising — soon da girl will be drowned (*He sees the stone idol*) She escape! (*He looks round in fury*) Where? How it happen?

Sinistro enters, dragging on the Princess

Sinistro Come, my proud beauty!
Princess I'll somehow get free, you see if I won't!
Sinistro And I'll use my magic to make sure you don't!
Crunchbones (*shouting*) Boodega! Nambo massemba!
Sinistro (*calmly; smoothly*) Ah, a native. Tell me my good man, how do I find the Shrine of Love?

Act I, Scene 3

Crunchbones Fool! Don't you talk to me like I am something under da nearest stone. I am da master heyah!
Princess Then set me free, *please!*
Crunchbones Who am you dat dares to talk to me?
Princess I am the Princess. And I will marry the Caliph of Constantinople, come what may!
Sinistro Quiet! (*To Crunchbones*) I might ask you the same, who are you that dares talk to *me*?
Crunchbones I am da Witchdoctor.
Sinistro (*craftily*) I also am a witchdoctor of a sort.
Crunchbones But you are not *good* witchdoctor so I don't tell you where da Shrine of Love is. You don't have my magic. I put da sacred bones on da ground and den you is in my power! (*He puts the bones on the ground*) Bowango!
Sinistro (*bored*) Oh yes, yes, yes — charming — (*To the struggling Princess*) Keep still you. (*To Crunchbones*) I have just asked you a question, so answer it. Where is the Shrine of Love?
Crunchbones You be silent, baggy pants! I not tell you!
Princess Allah be praised! The Witchdoctor is going to save me!
Crunchbones I save you all right — I save you for myself! (*To Sinistro*) I do not obey you! I only obey Bowango, da god of da sea! Dese are his sacred bones ...

He makes passes at the bones and there are tingling percussion effects

Sinistro (*sarcastically*) The god of the sea? We'll soon see about your god of the sea! (*He waves his arms, casting a spell at the stone idol*)

    Spirits of Darkness, I now demand
    You show this half wit who's in command!

Dramatic music chords, the Lights dim and the red eyes of the stone idol light up and then flicker. There are rumblings from percussion and thunder effects and the idol collapses in two. The Princess is scared and Crunchbones jabbers with fright and points to the wrecked idol

Crunchbones   Dulembo Yussambi! It is you dat rule!
                  For your gods are greater dan mine!
Sinistro   Then show me the way, you jabbering fool,
                  That will lead to the mystical Shrine!
Crunchbones   It is not far through da valley
                  You is dere by da sunset hour
Sinistro   And you will come along with me
                  For *I* am the one with the power.

Crunchbones bows, terrified

Crunchbones   It is so, oh master
                I have nodding left to say
                Except for "Boombah, Boombah"
                Which means dat I will obey.

Crunchbones collects up his bones

Princess (*wretchedly*) I thought you were going to help me!
Crunchbones (*sternly*) Boombah!
Princess Boombah? That's all you ever think about!
Crunchbones (*furiously*) Zug!

Crunchbones hustles her offstage, taking the bones with him

Sinistro (*to the Audience*) Everything's working out *beautifully*. Ha, ha, ha!

Sinistro exits

Two of the Nirvana Islanders (a boy and a girl) enter chattering noisily

Boy (*gesticulating*) Yombassi gooloo samani ...
Girl Tamboosi goomballa ...
Boy (*pointing*) The god of the sea!
Girl (*excitedly*) Bowango—he has been destroyed!
Boy (*excitedly*) Bowango destroyed! Maybe that means *happiness* will come to Nirvana!
Girl Happiness! We must tell the others! Happiness after all these years!
Boy Yes—we must go to the village—come!

They run off together, greatly excited

Sinbad and Talida enter in similar excitement

Sinbad What was the noise?
Talida The stone idol is broken—oh Sinbad, you have brought luck to my country!
Sinbad P'raps I have! And you've brought luck to me!
Talida What d'you mean?
Sinbad I've travelled all over the world and, until now, never fallen in love.
Talida (*laughing*) Then we need the *Shrine* of love!
Sinbad (*remembering; intensely*) That's right! It will be beautiful for *us* but terrible for the Princess! So how do we reach the Shrine?
Talida Through the Emerald Valley.
Sinbad Oh, that's all right then.
Talida But the Emerald Valley is watched over by a huge eagle! He is called the Giant Roc Bird and his nest is in the valley!
Sinbad Oh, that's good!
Talida He lives on human flesh.
Sinbad (*pulling a face*) Oh, that's bad! (*Unhappily*) That's very bad indeed.
Talida You're beginning to wish you had never come?
Sinbad If I hadn't come to Nirvana, I'd never have met you. Where is the Emerald Valley?
Talida (*pointing off*) You see the cliff by the sea?
Sinbad Yes!
Talida You see the hole in the cliff?
Sinbad Yes!
Talida That is the cave of the Old Man of the Sea—he is the Guardian of the Valley.

Act I, Scene 3

Sinbad It's a strange grotto.
Talida Well, he's a strange man. (*Anxiously*) He's crafty, he's cunning and he's cruel.
Sinbad I don't care!

They laugh at this, and hold hands

Upstage, Mrs Sinbad and Tinbad enter soppily, also hand in hand

Mrs Sinbad (*singing, unaccompanied*)
>"Take my hand,
>I'm a strange looking parasite."

Tinbad You can say that again! (*He sees the wrecked stone idol and is scared*) Look at that! It's one of the gods of the island but it's been destroyed! (*To the Audience*) I'm frightened! I'm frightened!
Audience Kismet!
Tinbad (*with a big smile, "thumbs up" sign*) Thanks—I'm better now!
Mrs Sinbad (*gazing round*) This place reminds me of that Greek island we went to on one of Sinbad's voyages.
Tinbad Which Greek island?
Mrs Sinbad Domestos.
Tinbad Oh see, it's Sinbad!
Mrs Sinbad Thank goodness we've found him!
Tinbad And *he's* found a girl! Who is it?
Mrs Sinbad She's got a grass skirt ... a flower in her hair ... it's Shirley Bassey!
Sinbad Hullo, Mum! Hullo, Tinbad! This is Talida.
Tinbad (*in a deep, solemn voice*) Take me to Ta ... lida.
Mrs Sinbad (*inspecting Talida*) Interesting ... what is it?
Sinbad I rescued her from the Witchdoctor.
Mrs Sinbad Which doctor?
Sinbad That's right.
Mrs Sinbad What d'you mean, that's right?
Sinbad (*explaining*) WITCH doctor, WITCH doctor.
Mrs Sinbad / **Tinbad** (*together*) (*pat-a-cake business with hands*) Witch doctor, witch doctor, all fall down.
Talida You are Sinbad's mother?
Mrs Sinbad (*aggressively*) Yes—and what about it?
Talida When you are so young?
Mrs Sinbad (*thrilled*) Oh! What a *nice* girl! I'm Semolina Sinbad and this is my steady, Tinbad the Tailor. ("*Girl to girl*") Isn't he a lovely hunk of man? I call him Chunky Chops 'cos he looks like the dog's dinner!
Tinbad (*to Talida*) I like your skirt—who made it—Percy Thrower?
Talida "Percythrowa"—she is good dress designer?
Sinbad (*laughing*) Talida has told me how to find the Shrine of Love, so now we're off to meet the Old Man of the Sea in his grotto!
Mrs Sinbad (*starting, dramatically*) *The Old Man of The Sea*? I once met a sailor who knew a poem about him. It's a bit scarey ...
Sinbad A poem? And why is it scarey?

Mrs Sinbad (*with more drama*) It just is ... er ... (*reciting*) "There's an old man of the sea, by everyone he's feared ... er ... er ..."
Tinbad   There's a funny old man in Darjeeling
             Who walks upside down on the ceiling
             There's some juice on his clothes
             And all up his nose
             Because of the orange he's peeling.
Mrs Sinbad (*hitting him with her handbag*) No, the poem's something to do with his beard ...
Talida He *has* got a beard, that is true! So tell us the poem!
Mrs Sinbad (*shaking her head*) Drat. I've forgotten it. It's gone.
Sinbad And so must we! Come on, Talida — to the Old Man's grotto.
Mrs Sinbad (*anxiously*) Be careful, dear — he's a nasty bit of work.
Tinbad (*calling*) If he lives near the sea, you must drop in!

Sinbad and Talida exit laughing

Mrs Sinbad (*watching them sentimentally*) I do believe they're in love!
Tinbad That reminds me. You and me all alone on a desert island, so ... (*singing unaccompanied*)

              "A sleepy lagoon
              A tropical moon
              And two on an island ..."

Mrs Sinbad Oh Gawd, he thinks he's Roy Plumley.
Tinbad (*taking her hand*) Semolina, can I have a kiss?
Mrs Sinbad No.
Tinbad Surely I can kiss your hand. (*He does so, elaborately*)
Mrs Sinbad Well kiss it, don't wash it. (*To the Audience*) The way he lingers over me fingers!
Tinbad My heart is cold. It needs to be warmed.
Mrs Sinbad Try a Mickey Mouse hot water bottle.
Tinbad You've no passion.
Mrs Sinbad I'm full of passion! I'm a woman, I've got a nice soft skin outside and inside my veins are dark and hot!
Tinbad You're not a woman, you're a black puddin'.
Mrs Sinbad Can't you say anything romantic?
Tinbad Yes. "Anything romantic".
Mrs Sinbad No, no, words of endearment.
Tinbad You are my peach, my plum, the apple of my eye.
Mrs Sinbad What am I — a fruit salad? Don't you remember, I was runner up in the Miss Constantinople Contest!
Tinbad Who was first?
Mrs Sinbad Hilda Ogden.
Tinbad Well, Hilda's a good cook! I will say that for her.
Mrs Sinbad (*indignantly*) So am I! Leave me for a minute and I'll prove it! I'll get some food for you!
Tinbad What, on this island?
Mrs Sinbad Certainly. I'm not just a pretty face you know.

Act I, Scene 3

Tinbad All right—*Choochie* Face! (*To the Audience*) I'd like something Arabian. I'd like a couple of sheep's eyes—they'd see me through the day.

Tinbad exits

Mrs Sinbad Oh what a hunk of man! I'm panting with passion! Mind you, with me, anyone in trousers bring out the pants! Oh, I'm in love! (*She sings*)

Song 7

At the second chorus of this disco song the Islanders suddenly pop out from the right wing on the "ooo-ooo-ooo" parts of the lyric and disappear again

During the rest of the lyric, two Islander girls or juveniles enter and stand each side of Mrs Sinbad

As she sings they do disco movements, banging their clenched hands together, then patting their cheeks

For the last "ooo-ooo-ooo" Mrs Sinbad expectantly turns to the right wing where the Islanders have been popping out, but they (this final time) pop out from the left wing instead and into the noisy coda for a

PRODUCTION NUMBER

After it, the Islanders exit

Mrs Sinbad (*remembering*) What am I doing? Here I am telling the world that I think Tinbad is a lovely fellar, when all the time I promised I'd find him some food! Oh, of course ... Why didn't I think of it before ...

She goes to the wings and collects a plastic bag with pheasant's feathers sticking out at one side

I bought this from Macfisheries for the voyage—such a nice man there—he knows I'm poor and he gave it me free! Oh I *know* Tinbad will like it. It's a beautiful pheasant, see!

Pleased, she opens the plastic bag to show the audience the bird. At once, her smile stops and she pulls a face

What a terrible smell! Oh, this is awful! Oh dear, this thing's been dead for years! What a perfectly putrid pong!

Tinbad returns

Tinbad (*rubbing his hands eagerly*) Got the food?
Mrs Sinbad Yes, dear. (*To the Audience*) Perhaps he won't notice.
Tinbad (*coyly*) Semolina, I want something from you!
Mrs Sinbad (*coyly*) And you're going to get it!
Tinbad You're going to give me the kiss?
Mrs Sinbad No. I'm going to give you the bird.
Tinbad What?
Mrs Sinbad My little joke. It's a pheasant! (*She gives him the plastic bag*)
Tinbad A pheasant? I *knew* you'd find some food, oh it is nice of you, Semolina, thank you very much.

Mrs Sinbad Not at all, dear. (*To the Audience*) I'd better leave him to it or he might turn nasty—like the pheasant!

Mrs Sinbad exits

Tinbad I say, isn't Mrs Sinbad super? Fancy giving me a lovely—(*He notices the smell*) Oh—oh—this bird's dead and gone and come back again! Oh... who can I give it to? (*He looks off*) Here comes Mustapha, I'll give it to him.

Mustapha enters

Tinbad Just the person I'm looking for!
Mustapha Well, *I'm* looking for food. I'm starving.
Tinbad How incredible! Because I've got a present for you.
Mustapha A present?
Tinbad It's the present of a pheasant.
Mustapha Oh, it's very pleasant to be given the present of a pheasant. Who's it from?
Tinbad A peasant.
Mustapha I might have guessed.
Tinbad Well, here you are, a nice pheasant—all you have to do is build a fire on the beach and cook it!

Tinbad exits, holding his nose

Mustapha Good old Tinbad. He and I have sailed together with Sinbad on every voyage. He's a real mate of mine and—(*He opens the bag and receives the smell full in the face*) Here, he's playing a trick on me! What a ghastly gas! Oh there's nothing else for it—I'll build a fire and *burn* it!

Mustapha exits with the bag, taking another peep inside, and then coughing and spluttering

And the other side Tinbad enters, laughing

Mrs Sinbad rushes on

Mrs Sinbad Oh Tinbad! Tinbad!
Tinbad What is it?
Mrs Sinbad (*looking round frantically*) Where have you put it? Where's the bag with the pheasant in it? I must get it! I've just remembered—that kind man at Macfisheries knows how poor we are and he put a *five pound note* in with the pheasant! It's in the bag!
Tinbad (*excitedly*) Five pound note in the bag?
Mrs Sinbad Yes!

Mustapha enters, holding the bag at arms length, pulling faces

Mustapha Oooooooooer ... a fire ... where can I light a fire ...?

Mustapha looks round. Mrs Sinbad rushes up to him and snatches the bag

Mrs Sinbad Don't worry, dear, don't worry—*I'll* take the pheasant!

Tinbad grabs the bag also and they tussle for it

Act I, Scene 3

Tinbad No, *I'll* take the pheasant! *I'll* take the pheasant!
Mrs Sinbad No, *I'll* take the pheasant! *I'll* take the pheasant!
Mustapha (*holding up the money*) Yes, and I'll take the *five pound note*!

There are yells of indignation from Mrs Sinbad and Tinbad who chase Mustapha off and all three exit to loud vauderville musical accompaniment

There is a Black-out

Scene 4

Outside the Grotto of the Old Man of the Sea (tabs or front-cloth)

Sinistro enters, dragging the Princess with him

Princess Let me go, you reptile! I demand to be set free—let me go!
Sinistro I shouldn't shout, my dear, there's no-one to hear you. (*He squeezes her arm tightly*)
Princess Ow—you're hurting me!
Sinistro I'm sorry, my precious. Twenty thousand pardons.
Princess (*fed up*) Oh it's too much . . .
Sinistro All right then, nineteen thousand.
Princess (*breaking away from him*) You're still hurting me!
Sinistro (*to the Audience*) I do dislike violence, but I'm awfully good at it.
Princess One day you'll pay for this! You're Ming the Merciless and Jack the Ripper rolled into one!
Sinistro (*pleased*) Yes, that's very true. I'm Arabia's answer to Vincent Price. Alas, we've no time for these compliments. We have to move on through the Emerald Valley, so first I have to talk to the Old Man of the Sea. I gather he's devious, dangerous and dirty—but he controls things round here. (*He is about to enter the cave, but stops*) Oh . . . don't run away, dearest. It would be brave but foolish to do that. On Nirvana there are gorillas and lions and snakes and if you do run away, they'll eat you! (*Over-acting dramatically*) In the tropical sunlight all looks peaceful and sublime, but in the dark grey misty shadows of this island there is disaster, disease and dreadful death. You know what I'm wanting now?
Princess Yes, an Oscar.
Sinistro No, I'm wanting to find the way through the Grotto so that we can reach the Shrine. (*To the Audience*) Everything's working out *beautifully*! (*Laughing evilly*) Ha, ha, ha . . .

Sinistro exits as the music for Song 8 begins

Princess (*over music*) I daren't disobey him . . . I'll have to wait for him here . . . last week I was in the Caliph's palace in Constantinople with a hundred servants! Today I am in this wretched place, and alone. Oh, to be back home with my beloved. (*She sings*)

Song 8

The Islanders can join in the Princess's song, unseen in the wings

After the song Sinistro enters from the Grotto

Sinistro All is well—and the Old Man of the Sea has told me interesting news. Sinbad has reached the island.
Princess (*delighted*) Sinbad has reached the island! Then I'll soon escape from your clutches! You can't watch over me every minute of the day, so I'll nip off when you're not looking!
Sinistro Are you trying to make a monkey out of me?
Princess No, Nature beat you to it.
Sinistro Your confidence is misplaced. The Old Man of the Sea has a secret that will prevent Sinbad from following us further.
Princess (*scared*) What secret?
Sinistro It's written in a poem but luckily no-one knows this poem.
Princess Then I am lost. What is to become of me?
Sinistro When we reach the Shrine of Love I'll tell you what is to become of you. You'll become "Mrs Sebastian Sinistro, the magician's assistant". There's a name to conjure with.
Princess Is that what happens if I drink the Waters of Eternity?
Sinistro (*nodding*) You will be compelled to fall in love with me.
Princess Never. I'm going no further. (*She turns away from him*)
Sinistro I think not, my dear. Look at me.

The Princess reluctantly looks at Sinistro

Watch this talisman. (*He holds up the jewel round his neck and swings it to and fro*)

The Princess watches it and is hypnotized

(*To the Audience*) And *you* watch what hypnosis can do. See, suddenly she is tired. She's so tired she could sleep on a clothes line. (*Chanting*) You will come with me . . .
Princess I will come with you . . .
Sinistro To the Emerald Valley . . .
Princess To the Emerald Valley . . .
Sinistro Through this sinister Grotto, dark and grey,
To the Valley of Emeralds, let us away!

He backs towards the Grotto entrance, swinging the jewel. The Princess follows, in a trance

The Princess passes Sinistro and exits

Sinistro (*to the Audience*) It's such fun being wicked! Oh, everything's working out *beautifully*. Ha, ha, ha, ha, ha!

Sinistro exits

Mysterious music is heard. The stage darkens, a green spotlight picks up the Old Man of the Sea as he quirkily pops his head round the Grotto entrance.

Act I, Scene 4

He is a slimy, eccentric, senile old man with a high pitched voice and he crawls on stage like a weird monkey, then stands up, his body remaining twisted

Old Man   Here among the seaweed and the slime
I know I look like Old Father Time
But I'm very old, I'm two hundred and three
And *I'm* the Old Man of the Sea.
If I was a human I'd go blotto
Living in a dark and dismal grotto
But it isn't so bad for the likes of me
There's a bed, a bath, separate W.C.
Now here's the thing you have to guess
Am I really wicked?

The Audience will say "yes"

That was a very cheeky reply. Any more replies like that and I'll turn you into jelly-fish, then tread on you! (*He cackles*) Squelch — yeuk! Yes, there's going to be a lot of trouble if you don't keep your measly little mouths shut, you ignorant humans. I may be old and twisted like a fig tree, but I still have some magic power and I shall —

Sinbad and Talida enter, talking together

(*Gasping*) That's the girl that the Witchdoctor offered as a sacrifice! This swashbuckling lad must have rescued her — I must keep my wits about me ... (*With great charm*) How do you do, young people, greetings from the humble Grotto of the poor Old Man of the Sea.
Sinbad (*cheerfully*) Greetings! (*To the Audience*) It's Father Christmas!
Talida (*scared*) That is the Old Man of the Sea!
Sinbad Well now I've seen him, I haven't a worry in the world! He's a dear old man! You run back to the others and tell them not to worry.
Talida But will you be all right?
Sinbad With this funny old boy? Of course!
Talida You're right, he can do you no harm. Though I wonder what his secret is ...
Sinbad His secret? Oh it's some old wives tale. You leave him to Sinbad the Sailor. This isn't the first time trouble has turned out to be nothing at all!
Talida (*laughing*) When he's told you how to reach the Emerald Valley, come and collect us.
Sinbad Of course.
Talida (*anxiously*) Sinbad—
Sinbad Now *don't* worry!

Talida smiles at Sinbad and exits

When she has gone the Old Man starts acting with great pathos

Old Man (*coughing*) Oh my throat ... I'm choking ... I'm so old I can hardly walk. (*He shuffles*) Only a few paces then I have to give up. (*He shuffles again*)
Sinbad You poor old man, I'll help you.

Old Man Er ... yes ... but *how* will you help me?
Sinbad Lean on me and we'll walk together.
Old Man I don't think I can manage that. I've got flat feet. I know! *Let me climb on your shoulders.*
Sinbad What?
Old Man Let me climb on your shoulders.
Sinbad But why?
Old Man (*pathetically*) My boy, I can't walk now, can I? I've got flat feet, like I said.
Sinbad Oh, we'll hobble along together.
Old Man (*with sudden blind fury; shouting*) LET ME CLIMB ON YOUR SHOULDERS!!!!

There is silence. Sinbad is now uncertain. He moves away

Sinbad (*aside to the Audience*) Bit funny, isn't he? D'you think I can trust him?
Audience No!
Sinbad No, I don't either.
Old Man (*whining*) I'm so old, so very old ... do you know when I went to school, I used to carry the books for a girl friend and if she were alive today she'd be one hundred and eighty seven!
Sinbad (*laughing; relaxed*) You're an incredible old boy! All right then, it'll be a bit of a lark. Up on my shoulders!

The innocent Sinbad bends down so that the Old Man can "piggy back" onto Sinbad's shoulders

Old Man Thank you, nice young Sinbad
For your kindness shown to me—
And soon you'll learn the secret
Of the Old Man of the Sea—ha, ha, ha! (*He cackles*)

The Old Man and Sinbad exit

Talida, Mrs Sinbad, Tinbad and Mustapha enter. Mrs Sinbad has a large handbag with her

Mustapha So now we're outside the Grotto ... (*He pulls a comically scared face*)
Mrs Sinbad (*exhausted*) Oh. I've just had to paddle through a pool with a sandy bottom. (*She turns upstage to look round at the location and we see a large orange mark on her seat*)
Tinbad Now she tells us!
Mrs Sinbad (*pointing offstage; amused*) Look, there's Sinbad with the Old Man of the Sea on his back.
Tinbad Ooooo—I don't like him. I'm frightened! I'm frightened!
Audience Kismet!
Tinbad (*giving the "thumbs-up" sign*) Thanks—I'm better now!
Mustapha Isn't that nice of him. He's a good lad, giving an OAP a lift like that.

Act I, Scene 4

Mrs Sinbad I wish I could remember the poem about the Old Man of the Sea.
Tinbad Ask Pam Ayres. (*He recites in a Mummerset accent*)
"I'll tell you a poem as quick as I can
It's all about a dirty old man."
Mrs Sinbad (*excitedly*) No, no, wait a minute! I think I remember the poem!
Talida Great!
Tinbad Excellent!
Mustapha Fantabulous!

All three listen earnestly

Mrs Sinbad   "The Old Man of the Sea,
(*reciting*)   By sailors he is feared
   He has the same amount of strength ..."

(*Her excitement tails off and she ends feebly*)

   ... da da, da da, da da ...

All three groan disappointedly

Sinbad Oh for Pete's sake ...
Mustapha You've got a memory like a sieve ...
Talida It's a shame ...
Mrs Sinbad I'm sorry, darlings. I got all worked up.
Tinbad All washed up, you mean. (*To the others*) Come on. (*He hits Mrs Sinbad*) Silly moo.
Mrs Sinbad Don't you hit me like that. I've said I'm sorry. If I can't remember, I can't remember. Forgetting things is a woman's purgative!

The four exit, the disgusted Tinbad pushing the complaining Mrs Sinbad off

Some sinister music as Sinbad enters, now a bit exhausted, still with the Old Man on his shoulders. He starts to cross the stage with his burden

Sinbad (*panting*) Ah ... ah ... Old Man of the Sea, don't hold on so tight!
Old Man (*evilly*) *Am* I holding on tight?
Sinbad Yes, you are. (*Frightened*) Here, just a minute, you're *tightening* your grip!
Old Man Tightening my grip? What do you mean?
Sinbad (*really scared*) Help! You're choking me! Help someone! Help!
Old Man   Now you *know* my secret
   And you thought you were so clever
   But you'll never get me off your back—
   Never, Never, NEVER!

Sinbad coughs and splutters and is forced to exit as the Old Man swipes him across the shoulder cruelly

Mrs Sinbad, Tinbad, Mustapha and Talida enter the other side

Mrs Sinbad "The Old Man of the Sea, by sailors he is feared, he has the same amount of strength—" What rhymes with feared?
Tinbad Weird?

Mustapha He's that all right. (*Pulling a face*) Really weird.
Talida Cleared?
Tinbad Jeered?
Mrs Sinbad (*shaking her head*) Leave me alone for a minute. I can think better when I'm on my own. (*Anxiously*) I'm sure Sinbad's in trouble.
Tinbad Of course he isn't! (*To the Audience*) Is Sinbad in trouble?
Audience Yes!
Mustapha In that case let's leave her to it and scarper!

He ushers Tinbad and Talida off, and they exit leaving a worried Mrs Sinbad behind

Mrs Sinbad I must remember it ... feared ... weird ...
Audience Beard!
Mrs Sinbad (*to the Audience*) What?
Audience Beard!
Mrs Sinbad That's it! *Beard*! (*She recites triumphantly*)
"The Old Man of the Sea
By sailors he is feared
He has the same amount of strength
AS HAIRS UPON HIS BEARD!"
That's it! (*She looks off and is at once scared*) Ooooooerrr! Here comes the old gargoyle! (*Calling out, trying not to show alarm*) Good morning! Nice day considering how hot it is!

Sinbad enters, staggering under the continuing weight of the Old Man

Sinbad (*gasping*) Oh – ah – oh – oh.
Old Man (*listening to his choking*) My friend has a bad cold! Heh, heh, heh.
Mrs Sinbad Sinbad, what's the matter with you dear? Throw the old man off!
Old Man (*laughing*) They all say that! But he can't! He can't! Hee, hee, hee!
Mrs Sinbad (*horrified*) I remember what happens! You stay up on their shoulders till they *die*! You keep them walking till they die of exhaustion! You pretend you're weak but you've got the strength of fifteen men!
Old Man Twenty!
Mrs Sinbad Well *I* know the rhyme about you! The only trouble is that I don't understand it. "He has the same amount of strength, as hairs upon his beard."
Old Man (*frightened*) My beard has nothing to do with it!
Mrs Sinbad Of *course*! To cut off your beard means to cut off your strength!
Old Man Stay away!

Mrs Sinbad opens her big handbag and takes out a pair of garden shears

Mrs Sinbad It's time for a shave!
Old Man Rubbish, you can't scare me!
Mrs Sinbad I can. It's a Wilkinson Blade.
Old Man (*panicking*) A Wilkinson Blade? No, no, don't cut off my beard!

Act I, Scene 4   31

Mrs Sinbad (*advancing on him with the shears*) Then slide off my son's back at once!
Old Man Yes, of course, of course. (*He gets off Sinbad and cringes*) Don't cut off my beard! I'm a poor old man, a lonely poor old man ...
Sinbad holds his hands to his throat and chokes and gasps, trying to recover
Mrs Sinbad (*calling*) Talida! Tinbad! Mustapha!
Talida, Tinbad and Mustapha enter
Sinbad is still coughing and Talida comforts him
Talida Sinbad!
Sinbad (*croaking; hoarse*) I'm all right ... What a horrible old man, he nearly killed me.
Tinbad (*eyes popping at the thought; turning to the Audience*) He nearly killed him! I'm frightened! I'm frightened!
Audience Kismet!
Tinbad ("*thumbs-up*" *sign to the Audience*) Thanks — I'm better now!
Mrs Sinbad (*indignantly*) Killed you? Then put the pressure on — make him help us!
Sinbad Good idea. (*Sternly; to the Old Man*) Show us the way to the Shrine of Love.
Old Man No.
Mrs Sinbad (*stepping towards him with the shears*) Yes!
Old Man (*scared*) Spare me! I'll do anything if you'll spare me!
All Thank you very much.

Sinbad begins the song, then Talida, Mrs Sinbad, Mustapha and Tinbad join in

                                    Song 9

Sinbad   You'll help us, you say,
                           So give us a sign,
                           And show us the way
                           To the magical Shrine!
Old Man It's through the Grotto where I live!

The Old Man waves his hands as though casting a spell, and thus ushers in the change of scene

(*Calling out and waving his arms*) The Grotto of Living Statues!
All the others (*calling out and waving their arms, but frightened*) The Grotto of Living Statues!

Dramatic music and the frontcloth is flown or tabs open

Scene 5(a)

The Grotto of Living Statues

In the Grotto are various coral pink stalagmite rocks of different heights. On them, still as statues, stand three men and three girls. Over their faces and bodies are dark grey and off-white scrim – like veils of straggling lengths of net. The scene is dimly lit, and is not like an attractive Transformation Scene but is weird and spooky

Sinbad (*aghast*) Living statues!

They wander round apprehensively looking at the strange immobile figures

Mustapha They're rolling stones!
Mrs Sinbad They're made of punk rock!
Mustapha (*examining them*) No, they're coral – what d'you know about coral?
Tinbad She lives at number six, next to Mrs Mazouk. You should see her in her black leather and green hair – she's a little raver. (*He bumps into a statue*) Ach – spooky statue! I'm frightened! I'm frightened!
Audience Kismet!
Tinbad (*"thumbs-up" to them*) Thanks – I'm better now!
Old Man They've all disobeyed me, so here they dwell!
And I've made their life a living hell!

The Old Man cackles with pleasure at the thought but Sinbad is enraged

Sinbad You have been evil, so to atone
Set them free from this curse of stone!
Old Man (*cowering with fear*) Whatever you say, oh master. (*He waves his arms about, casting a spell*)
Abracadabra, Abracadee
Living statues, I set you free!
Sinbad That's better!

There is a chord and the statues slowly move and we hear ratchet percussion effects and rumbling music as they awaken. They stretch themselves and turn to Sinbad, calling out over the continuous awaking music as they come to life in a spooky, ghoulish, Frankenstein style

1st Statue (*loudly*) Blessings upon you, oh Master Sinbad!
2nd Statue Our gratitude is eternal!
3rd Statue Our thanks are as many as the sands of time!
4th Statue Allah is merciful and Sinbad is his servant!
1st Statue (*to Mrs Sinbad*) The blessings of Heaven fall upon your head and may you have a hundred children!
Mrs Sinbad By Allah, I hope not!
2nd Statue We all sing the praises of the boy who is the son of Mrs Sinbad!
Mrs Sinbad Here – I should hope so – whose boy did you think he was? I'm not staying here to be insulted.
Tinbad Well, if you want to be insulted somewhere else, where shall we go?

Act I, Scene 5

Talida Let us see the rest of the Grotto!
Mustapha Yes — we can see some sea shells on the sea shore, surely!
Mrs Sinbad Say that again.
Mustapha We can see shome shee shells on the shee . . . I can't!

The Old Man points to the statues who are now exercising themselves

Old Man   While the blood returns to their frozen veins,
              Let me show you my coral domains —
Mrs Sinbad   And I bet they smell of nasty drains!

Mrs Sinbad, Tinbad and Mustapha exit with Sinbad, Talida and the Old Man

The Music for Song 10 starts and although it is probably a pop song the choreography is stylized and shows the Statues coming to life

Spirits of the Grotto enter and join the Production Number

Song 10

After this routine, the principals — except Sinbad — return, ushered in by the Old Man

Old Man   Beyond the Emerald Valley
              Where the Roc Bird flies
              There you will find the magic Shrine
              And the Waters of Paradise!

There is a fanfare, and Sinbad enters in a magnificent turban and cloak, holding a huge silver scimitar

Sinbad   Old Man of the Sea
              No more shilly-shally
              Show us now the magical gates
              That lead to the Emerald Valley!
Old Man (*cringing*) You spared my life, oh master, so I must obey! (*He makes magical passes towards the rear of the Grotto*)

There is a fanfare with rumbling percussion effects, and either the backcloth is flown or the rocks part. We see a bright and dazzling Magnificent Gateway

SCENE 5(b)

The Gates to the Emerald Valley

All sing the last eight bars of the Theme Song (reprise)

Song 6 (reprise)

A Grand Tableau is now staged. Posed are Mrs Sinbad, Tinbad, Talida, Mustapha, the Old Man of the Sea, the Living Statues and Spirits of the Grotto — and centre stage is Sinbad posed dramatically on a stalagmite rock, holding the huge scimitar on high

CURTAIN

ACT II

Scene 1

The nest of the Giant Roc Bird in the Emerald Valley

As the Curtain *rises loud bird noises and suitable music is heard*

The young Chorus, dressed as exotic birds, come round from each side of the huge nest for their dance routine

Song 11

After the dance the "birds" exit

The Islanders, in exotic costumes, enter to solemn music, carrying trays and baskets of food which they lay on the ground ceremoniously in front of the giant nest

1st Islander Pineapples and bananas for the Giant Roc Bird!
2nd Islander Peaches and hibiscus blossom salad for the Giant Roc Bird!
3rd Islander Poi poi fruit and Roc cakes for the Giant Roc Bird!
4th Islander Sometimes he flies here at early morn!
5th Islander Sometimes the Giant Roc is here by midday!
6th Islander Sometimes he arrives at the setting of the sun!

They chant solemnly

All   At one o'clock, at two o'clock, at three o'clock, Roc!
        Four o'clock, five o'clock, six o'clock Roc!
        Seven o'clock, eight o'clock, nine o'clock, Roc!
        We're gonna rock around the clock tonight!

The tempo takes over and they gradually slide into singing

Song 11(A)

The young Chorus, as "birds" enter and join in

After the number there is a crash from percussion and Crunchbones leaps on stage

Everyone bows to Crunchbones in fear

All Wallah!
Crunchbones Wallah! Wallah, boombah! Islanders, has I got time to cross dis Emerald Valley before da Giant Roc Bird arrives?
1st Islander Yes, O Witchdoctor.
Crunchbones Good. Den all is satisfactory.

Act II, Scene 1

2nd Islander (*scared*) But the Roc Bird will return soon!
Crunchbones Ho Ho! We shall have gone by den. (*Gloating*) But Sinbad and his stupid friends will still be heyah and (*with a swooping gesture, his hand like a claw*) da Roc Bird will swoop down on dem and grab dem. (*To the Audience*) You remember da film called *Jaws*? Well dis will be "Claws" — and dat's far worse! (*He closes his claw-like hand and makes a blood-thirsty noise*) Kkkkrrrcccch! (*Delighted*) Dat will be de end of dem!
3rd Islander The Roc Bird, will he spare us?
4th Islander (*pointing*) We have put the food ready for him.
Crunchbones Den maybe he will spare you. Always remember dis, oh Natives of Nirvana. If you ever forget to bring da food to da nest, dere will be TERRIBLE trouble, it will be FEARFUL.
All Woe ... woe ... (*They all raise their hands*)
Crunchbones Cos if da Roc Bird find dere is no food to eat, den he will eat ... YOU.
All (*terrified*) Wallah!
Crunchbones You return to da village now. Your duty is done. (*Dismissively*) Boombah!
All Wallah!

The Islanders exit

Crunchbones (*beckoning offstage*) Come, Sinistro! Come, Princess! Dere is no need to fear ... yet.

Sinistro enters holding the hand of the Princess

Sinistro Soon we'll reach the Shrine. Come, beloved!
Princess I am not your beloved, nor ever shall be. (*Seeing the jewels*) Oh, what beautiful jewels!
Sinistro (*greedily*) Emeralds! We're in the Emerald Valley. Oh, but what do I want with jewels — I have my own jewel, she is here! (*He moves to her and tries to embrace her*)
Princess Go away you slimy toad.
Sinistro You won't say that once you have drunk the Waters of Eternity in the Shrine of Love.
Crunchbones (*laughing*) No, she will not! Ho, ho, ho.
Princess And you shut up as well, rumble belly.
Crunchbones What?
Princess I'll never drink the Waters of Eternity. Never, never, never.
Sinistro We shall see about that. What is that incredible nest?
Crunchbones Dat is da nest of da Giant Roc Bird. He returns to it every day — and if a human happens to be near, he sometimes eats dem. Oh woe.
Sinistro Then we must away! Come, Loved One.
Princess I would prefer to be eaten by the Roc Bird than be loved by you.
Crunchbones Hey! No time to argue! We go now before da Roc Bird comes!
Princess I will stay and face this danger.
Sinistro Your pride is beautiful but ... (*gazing at her*) Look at me.
Princess No. I only obey the Caliph of Constantinople.
Sinistro (*with a hand gesture*) Look at me!!!

There are strange percussion sounds. The Princess looks at Sinistro and he hypnotizes her with the magic gestures. Crunchbones watches fascinated

Crunchbones (*admiringly to the Audience*) He make good magic. (*He nods his head wisely*) Really professional.
Sinistro (*continuing the gestures*) Your self-will is draining away from your body and you are compelled to obey. (*To the Audience*) Watch my technique carefully—I make Svengali look like Little Noddy. (*To the Princess*) You will obey!
Princess (*trance-like*) I will obey.
Crunchbones   She look at him like he was a genie!
   He just as good as da Great Houdini!
Sinistro (*to the Princess*) You will follow ...
Princess (*trance-like*) I will follow ...

The Princess watches Sinistro's magic gestures, passes him and exits in a daze as he recites

Sinistro   Soon the Roc Bird will fly down from above
   And we will be safe in the Shrine of Love!
Crunchbones   But Sinbad and his friends will be heyah
   And dey will die—oh deyah, oh deyah! (*He makes the claw swooping gesture and the "Kkkkrrrccch" noise again*)
Sinistro (*delighted; to the Audience*) Everything's working out *beautifully*! Ha, ha, ha!
Crunchbones (*with the same intonation*) Ho, ho, ho!

The two villains laugh as they exit after the Princess

Mrs Sinbad and Tinbad enter with a large picnic basket

Tinbad   It is hot! It's a hundred and twenty degrees in the shade!
Mrs Sinbad   Ah, but *I'm* clever. I keep out of the shade.

Tinbad indicates to the Audience that Mrs Sinbad is stupid

Mrs Sinbad begins to unpack the basket

Tinbad (*pointing to the nest; scared*) Look at that nest! It must be for the biggest budgie in the world! I'm frightened! I'm frightened!
Audience   Kismet!
Tinbad (*with a big smile and "thumbs-up" sign*) Thanks—I'm all right now!
Mrs Sinbad (*pointing to the food offerings*) Whatever's on those plates?
Tinbad   Bananas and coconuts.
Mrs Sinbad   That's funny. Last year I went on a diet of bananas and coconuts.
Tinbad   What happened?
Mrs Sinbad   Well I didn't lose any weight but I could swing from tree to tree like nobody's business.
Tinbad (*examining them*) How do native dishes compare with ours?
Mrs Sinbad   Oh they break just as easily. (*She gazes around*) Isn't it romantic here ...

Act II, Scene 1

Tinbad (*gazing around*) So this is the car park behind Sainsbury's... (*or local reference*)
Mrs Sinbad And it's a lovely place for a picnic! (*She goes to the basket*)
Tinbad Ah — food — we'll show the world we're a good pair of picnickers.

Mrs Sinbad bends down with her back to the Audience and reveals her pink bloomers

I said picnickers not pink knickers!
Mrs Sinbad Sorry, dear. Spread the tablecloth.

She hands him a tablecloth and returns to scrummaging in the picnic basket. Tinbad lays the tablecloth on the ground

(*Taking them out of the basket*) Here we are — Marrowbone, Pal, Chappie, Winalot, Bonio, Whiskas Supermeat, McDougall's Saucy Sponge, a big bottle of salad oil, lettuce, rolls — (*she takes out toilet rolls*) — Oh, I packed the wrong rolls!

Tinbad turns away from the tablecloth

Tinbad Have you a thermos flask?
Mrs Sinbad I couldn't find one.
Tinbad Have you tried Boots?
Mrs Sinbad Yes, but the tea comes out of the holes.

The tablecloth whizzes off into the wings (on a nylon wire) unseen by either of them. Swanee whistle sound as it goes

Mrs Sinbad Have you laid the tablecloth like I said?
Tinbad Yes.
Mrs Sinbad (*turning to where the cloth should be*) Where?
Tinbad What you mean, where?
Mrs Sinbad The tablecloth's gone.
Tinbad Funny...
Mrs Sinbad It wasn't laid in the first place.
Tinbad Oh, yes it was.
Mrs Sinbad Oh, no it wasn't. (*To the Audience*) It wasn't there, was it?
Audience (*encouraged by Tinbad*) Oh, yes it was!
Mrs Sinbad Oh, no it wasn't.
Audience Oh, yes it was.
Mrs Sinbad Wasn't.
Audience Was.
Mrs Sinbad All right, I believe you — luckily I brought another.

She hands the second tablecloth to Tinbad and turns back to rummage in the basket. Tinbad lays the cloth on ground

Looking directly at the Audience, Mrs Sinbad holds up some food product and does whatever is the most daft commercial on T.V. at the moment

Tinbad has laid the cloth and now turns upstage. The second cloth whizzes offstage and the swanee whistle is heard again

Tinbad I've laid the tablecloth.
Mrs Sinbad Well, so long as you haven't laid anything else! (*She laughs merrily, then stops as she sees the tablecloth has gone*) The tablecloth's gone again.
Tinbad But I put it on the ground, it was grounded!
Mrs Sinbad Well, it's taken off!
Tinbad Funny ...
Mrs Sinbad It wasn't there in the first place.
Tinbad Oh, yes it was.
Mrs Sinbad Now don't let's start all that again. Luckily I brought another and *I'll* lay it this time so that nothing can go wrong. (*She takes the third tablecloth from the basket, hands it to Tinbad and also takes out a large hammer. Grimly*) I'm not going to be defeated by a tablecloth. So I'll spread it and you nail it down.
Tinbad Right. (*He starts to hammer noisily*)
Mrs Sinbad No, no, do it properly. When I nod my head, you hit it.
Tinbad What?
Mrs Sinbad When I nod my head, you hit it.
Tinbad But—(*he looks at the Audience*)
Mrs Sinbad Stop answering back and do as I say.
Tinbad Right! If that's what you want, I'm ready!

Mrs Sinbad nods her head. Tinbad hits her. There are percussion effects

Mrs Sinbad Ow! What d'you think you're doing?
Tinbad Knocking on wood! Ha, ha, ha, ha!

Unseen by them, the third cloth whizzes offstage, with swanee whistle effect

Mrs Sinbad (*furiously*) It's disappeared! I paid a lot of money for that one, I bought it off Elizabeth Taylor.
Tinbad Well, it's gone for a Burton.
Mrs Sinbad There's something spooky about this place. (*She takes a transistor radio from the picnic basket*) I'm going to cheer myself up with the radio. There's a programme about picnics on Woman's Hour. (*She switches the radio on*)

A voice is heard from the radio (either live at offstage mike or recorded)

Radio Voice This is Radio Four.
Mrs Sinbad Radio what?
Radio Voice Radio Four, fat head.
Mrs Sinbad (*addressing the radio*) Well, I only asked a civil question. Sorry!
Radio Voice Granted.

Mrs Sinbad turns away upstage and helps Tinbad take various other foods from the basket such as lettuce and cheese (overlarge size)

Tinbad (*holding up a kettle from the basket*) I'll go and fill this from the river.
Mrs Sinbad (*pointing off*) All right, dear, it's over there.

Act II, Scene 1

Mrs Sinbad and Tinbad both go over to the wings and look offstage, away from the radio

Radio Voice This programme is about slimming. We've had many letters from listeners asking how to get rid of the roll of fat round your waist. Well, that roll of fat *can* be got rid of.

Tinbad exits

Mrs Sinbad, not having heard the last radio speech, returns to the basket and takes out a French loaf

Mrs Sinbad Ah, here's the roll!
Radio Voice So, you must get rid of your roll as soon as you can.
Mrs Sinbad I don't want to do anything of the sort — this is a picnic!
Radio Voice Just get hold of the roll with both hands and hold tight — life isn't a picnic, you know.
Mrs Sinbad Well, I say it is! (*She holds on tightly to the roll but she is a bit mystified*)
Radio Voice Now, even though it may hurt, hit it hard.
Mrs Sinbad Hit it hard?
Radio Voice Smack it.
Mrs Sinbad (*shrugging*) She must be mad. (*She smacks the roll with her hand*)
Radio Voice Now get some oil and massage it into the roll.
Mrs Sinbad (*taking the bottle of salad oil*) I *was* going to put the oil on the salad . . . still, she knows best . . . (*She undoes the bottle and pours oil onto the roll*)
Radio Voice Rub it in hard.
Mrs Sinbad Right. Maybe it'll taste quite nice! (*She rubs oil into the roll*)
Radio Voice Now, here is the way to get rid of that roll of yours.
Mrs Sinbad Oh, I know how to get rid of a roll — eat it!
Radio Voice The way to get rid of a roll is simple. Stop eating.
Mrs Sinbad (*freezing in amazement*) Stop eating?
Radio Voice But for the moment, all you do is pat it.
Mrs Sinbad Bat with it? (*Uncertain, she holds the long roll like a cricket bat*)
Radio Voice Pat really well. Now, if you cheat, it isn't cricket, is it?
Mrs Sinbad I suppose not, no. But I like cricket, I played it at (*local school*).
Radio Voice So when you pat, pat hard.
Mrs Sinbad Of course! All cricketers do!
Radio Voice And as you pat, sway your body from side to side. That's it, let it all go free.

Mrs Sinbad looks blank, shrugs then attempts to sway

Radio Voice That's it. Wobble, wobble, wobble, come on, ladies!

Tinbad returns with the kettle and amazed, watches Mrs Sinbad wobbling about

That's it ladies, wobble, wobble, wobble!
Tinbad What on earth are you doing?

Mrs Sinbad Listening to the radio!
Radio Voice Go on — that's right — now have a ball!
Mrs Sinbad She wants us to play cricket but we haven't *got* a ball!
Tinbad We could use the buns.
Mrs Sinbad Good idea, there's some in the basket.
Radio Voice Now exercise. Try lifting your arms — go on, try some over-arm movements!

Tinbad picks up some buns and bowls one over his head

Tinbad Over-arm? I always do!
Radio Voice Now, next time you have a pat, try a stroke with your hand.
Mrs Sinbad Right! (*She practises a bat stroke with the roll*)
Tinbad I'm going to enjoy this!
Mrs Sinbad Bowl me a bun!

Tinbad does so (percussion effects here). Mrs Sinbad hits the bun into the Audience, then hits several more and the Audience throws them back

Radio Voice (*heartily*) Now for a nice hot bath!
Mrs Sinbad Hot bath? What's she talking about?
Tinbad I don't know! She's bananas!
Radio Voice This is the BBC, don't be cheeky.
Tinbad Same to you with nobs on! (*He switches off the radio indignantly*)

A few bars of Arabian music are heard and a Camel enters, making a loud whinnying noise

Mrs Sinbad What's that?
Tinbad Oh look — a horse with an air lock!
Mrs Sinbad It's Red Rum!
Tinbad It's Arkle!

The Camel stamps its feet and shakes his head

Mrs Sinbad It's getting the hump. Better be friendly with it — go and shake hands.

The Camel turns round as Tinbad crosses and holds out his hand. He finds himself shaking its tail

Tinbad If I'm shaking its hand, it's got a very funny face.
Mrs Sinbad Yes, but what *is* it? (*To the Audience*) All right then, all you clever chops, what is it?
Audience A camel!
Mrs Sinbad I love them! I could eat them all day!
Tinbad Not a caramel, a camel, stupid.
Mrs Sinbad Oh, a camel stupid. What an interesting creature.
Tinbad IT'S A CAMEL.
Mrs Sinbad WELL, DON'T SHOUT.

The Camel starts to sway

Tinbad Look, it's got indigestion.

Act II, Scene 1   41

Mrs Sinbad (*chanting*) "Setlers bring express relief ... Setlers bring express relief ..."
Tinbad (*to the Camel*) Then if it isn't indigestion, what are you doing? (*He puts his ear to the Camel's mouth, listening*) You're *dancing*?

The Camel nods

Where did you learn dancing? (*He listens to the Camel*) He says Mecca.

The Camel does a swinging action

Mrs Sinbad He learnt that movement from Lionel Blair.

The Camel turns round and swings its bottom

Tinbad And he learnt *that* one from Joyce Blair.
Mrs Sinbad Let's join him. Come on! After all he is a *hoofer*!

The percussion which accompanied the Camel's movements becomes the intro to Song 12. The Camel moves between Tinbad and Mrs Sinbad and they dance a soft shoe shuffle as they sing

Song 12

After the song all three exit

The Theme Music plays and Sinbad enters, holding Talida's hand

Sinbad (*looking around, pleased*) The Old Man of the Sea said when we leave the Grotto we must go East.
Talida That way is East. (*She points offstage*)
Sinbad Can you see the Shrine of Love?
Talida (*looking off*) No ... (*She sees the emeralds*) Oh, but Sinbad—look—I thought they were just green rocks but they're emeralds! See! (*She crouches down*)
Sinbad You look at the emeralds—I'll go and look for the Shrine. (*He points off*) I know, I'll climb that rock over there. Will you be all right?
Talida With all the jewels to play with? You must be joking.

They both laugh

Sinbad exits

Two young Islanders enter and bow to Talida

1st Islander
2nd Islander } (*together*) Nanua Talida!
Talida (*bowing back*) Nanua!
1st Islander (*pointing offstage*) Who was that?
Talida That's Sinbad the Sailor. (*Romantically*) He's good and kind and reckless and brave!
1st Islander (*to 2nd Islander*) She's in love with him.
2nd Islander Yes. (*Sympathetically*) Poor soul. (*To Talida*) Did you tell him about the evils of this island?
Talida I told him about the High Priestess and the Strange Man-Eating

Plant but I try to make light of these things. He's here to rescue the Princess so I only say nice things to him.
Both juveniles Happy talk?
Talida Exactly. (*She sings Song 13*)

Song 13

The Islanders can accompany Talida's song by performing Hawaiian-style hand movements

> *After the song the Islanders exit*
>
> *A tom-tom is heard and Crunchbones enters*

Crunchbones (*to the Audience*) Dat girl! Just ma luck — ho, ho, ho! (*He looks upwards*) Ah grab her before da Roc Bird arrives!

He creeps up behind Talida and claps his hand over her mouth. She struggles

> Yes, plump little maiden, it am Crunchbones da Witchdoctor. You escape from da Sacrifice Stone but you don't escape dis time! Oh goody, goody no! My wicked friends at da Shrine of Love will see to dat!

Crunchbones exits with the struggling Talida

Sinbad enters

Sinbad Isn't it great! I can see the roof of the Shrine! (*He looks around*) Talida? Oh, I know what's happened, she's gone further down the valley to find some emeralds. (*To the Audience*) What's that? You mean she *isn't* down the valley? You mean she *isn't* that way?
Audience No!
Sinbad Then is she *that* way? (*Points other way*)
Audience Yes? Witchdoctor! (*etc*)

Sinbad continues to question the Audience about Talida

> *Mrs Sinbad, Tinbad and Mustapha enter*

Mrs Sinbad What's all this noise about?
Tinbad Sounds like (*local football ground*) on a Saturday afternoon!
Sinbad My friends have just told me the most terrible news!
Mrs Sinbad Don't tell me — *Crossroads* is coming off.
Sinbad Worse than that.
Mustapha They've cancelled the Muppets!
Sinbad (*desperately*) The Witchdoctor has kidnapped Talida!
Tinbad That means he's taken her to the Shrine of Love!
Mrs Sinbad Well, I do want to bash on through the jungle with you dear, but my plates of meat ... (*She holds up her foot and massages her ankle*)
Sinbad Oh, Mum, come on! We must rescue her! (*Listening*) What's that?

A wind effect is heard, then dramatic music (No. 14 — no vocal needed)

Voice Off (*crowing loudly into mike*) Caw! Caw!
Mrs Sinbad (*to Tinbad*) You do make funny noises when you've got indigestion, dear.

Act II, Scene 1   43

Tinbad I haven't got indigestion.
Mrs Sinbad Talking of noises ... (*She continues to chatter*)

Terrified Islanders enter upstage, pointing melodramatically up to the sky

The four Principals are unaware of the Islanders' entry

... that noise reminds me of when we all had Dutch cheese, a Spanish omelette, German sausages and Italian pizza washed down with Russian vodka!
Mustapha Well I had Scotch broth with Irish stew and Chinese take-away.
Mrs Sinbad Ah, those were the days!
Tinbad Those were the nights as well.

The offstage wind noise, the "cawing" and the dramatic music are thunderously loud now. Strobe lighting starts and the Islanders become petrified as they point upwards, following the "flight" of the Giant Bird but our friends are still unaware

Islanders (*calling*) The Giant Roc! Boombah! Wallah! Spare us, oh winged one! Woe!

Still upstage, the Islanders kneel and salaam as the Giant Roc Bird arrives (see Scenery notes). Suddenly the four Principals see the arrival and yell the place down, shrieking over the music and cries of the Islanders

Sinbad The Roc Bird! We must get out of here fast!
Tinbad Blimey the Bird! (*To the Audience*) I'm frightened, I'm frightened!
Audience Kismet!
Tinbad ("*thumbs-up*" *to them*) Thanks — I'm all right now! ... I think! (*He sees the Bird*) Oooooo-er!
Mustapha Spare us!
Mrs Sinbad Run!! We're getting the bird!

The four scramble off, bumping into each other in fright as the sound effects and dramatic music become double forte

Islanders (*loudly*) O gods of the island, hear us! Have mercy! Save us! Help! Free us from this fate! Nirvana! Nirvana! Woe!

Black-out

Scene 2

The Jungle of Man-Eating Plants near the Shrine

The scene opens to bird song and jungle noises. The lighting is dim

Sinistro, laughing evilly, enters. He beckons, magically, offstage, and the Princess enters in a trance

Sinistro See — the Princess is under my fluence! Oh I'm a contented conjuror

... a satisfied sorcerer ... a happy medium. Oh I'm such a success aren't I? (*To the Audience's inevitable reaction*) Oh shurrup. (*He snaps his fingers in front of the Princess's face and she comes to*)

Sinistro Smile, oh subject of all my dreams!
Princess Never, oh object of all my nightmares.
Sinistro Come, come. Most people find me a very handsome man. (*To the Audience*) For instance you do, don't you?
Audience No! Get lost! (*etc.*)
Sinistro (*smugly ignoring this*) There, I told you they did.
Princess I must confess, I do like your beard ...
Sinistro (*to the Audience*) Aha! She likes my beard. I'm not surprised. It always gets them, you know.
Princess It's just the sort of beard that's right ... (*loudly*) for pulling! (*She pulls at his beard*)
Sinistro AAAAH! (*Threateningly*) You'll live to regret that. (*He casts his magic at her — percussion effects — and she goes into a trance again*)
(*reciting*) She is the King of Arabia's daughter
But wait till she swallows the magic water!
We'll soon reach the Shrine, and then just you see,
One sip of the water, and she will *love* me!

The Princess exits, ushered out by Sinistro

Sinistro turns to the Audience

Everything's working out *beautifully*. Ha, ha, ha!

Sinistro exits

Crunchbones enters with Talida, who struggles so much that Crunchbones has to put his bones on the ground

Talida Take that! (*She hits him*) And that! (*She hits him again*) Third time lucky! (*She hits his stomach*) One for the pot!
Crunchbones Ow! You one for da pot unless you behave! I had a big pot made for missionary many years ago.
Talida (*scared*) Then you're a cannibal!
Crunchbones (*nodding proudly*) Yes. When *I* go into a restaurant, I order da waiter. And I remember missionary. He make good soup, but he was tough. But you — you *plump* and *tasty*.
Talida Sinbad will catch us up and rescue me!
Crunchbones Sinbad will catch us up but he don't rescue *nobody*.
Talida I will fight you, and Sinbad will fight Sinistro!
Crunchbones But who will fight *Bludruncolda*?
Talida (*scared*) Bludruncolda?
Crunchbones Dat lady is da Priestess at da Shrine of Love. She cold lady, cold like da choc ice, 'cos she got no heart but much cruel magic.
Talida Three of you against me. All is lost.
Crunchbones Yes, my plump little boiling fowl, all is lost. So come!
Talida It is the end for me.
Crunchbones   Ho, ho, ho! Look what I've got!

Act II, Scene 2

(*to the Audience*) If she don't behave I put her in da pot!

Crunchbones drags the defeated Talida off

Mustapha enters from the other side

Mustapha (*looking round*) The island of Nirvana. Well, it's nothing like Thomas Cook described it. (*He sees the pile of bones*) Oh look, a pile of bones! I kernow what's kergoing to happen kernow—kersomebody is going to kermake some Knorr soup! (*He stops laughing, realizes*) Hey, they're very *big* bones. (*Unhappily*) Oooooer, I think they're *human* bones. (*He picks them up*) But whoever would carry those round with him? The Witchdoctor? Oh, but he's miles away! He's over the other side of the island! (*With bravado*) If I ever see him face to face... that great big slimy slab of jet black lard...

Crunchbones enters upstage and goes behind Mustapha, towering over him

... I'll go up to the fat little man and I'll say—(*seeing him*)—HELP!

Crunchbones Boombah! Kallawi boombah, bogo, bogo!

Mustapha studies Crunchbones as he waves his arms about fiercely

Mustapha Wait a minute. Haven't I seen you on a jar of marmalade?

Crunchbones (*furiously*) Boolah! You white man. And me *hate* white man. Dere is too many white men on dis island.

Mustapha (*to the Audience*) It's Enoch Powell. (*He laughs*) Enoch Powell! Ha, ha, ha!!! Oh that laugh's given me back my confidence! Now I can kill cruel cannibals, knife nasty natives, set Nirvana free and—

Crunchbones (*shouting*) BOOMBAH!

The startled Mustapha throws the pile of bones in the air in terror. Crunchbones picks them up

(*Sternly*) Me am Crunchbones da Witchdoctor, da cleverest man in da jungle.

Mustapha Then tell me—what do you call an elephant that flies?

Crunchbones (*blankly*) Elephant dat flies?

Mustapha A jumbo jet! (*He carries on triumphantly and points to one of the bones Crunchbones has picked up*) And what time is it when an elephant sits on one of those bones?

Crunchbones (*fed up*) Time to hit you on da head with one of dem. BOOMBAH! (*He hits Mustapha on the head with a bone*)

Mustapha stands still, gormless and cross-eyed

> Dere! Dat will make your toenails curl.
> And now to go back to ma beautiful girl.
> Dere's she and da Princess and ma Sorcerer friend—
> We soon reach da Shrine, and da journey's end!
> Ho, ho, ho, ho!

Crunchbones exits

Mustapha remains still as a statue

Sinbad enters and backs into Mustapha

Mustapha (*recovering*) } (*together*) { Oh!
Sinbad (*surprised*)
Mustapha (*feeling his head*) I do feel funny. I feel as if someone bashed me on the bonce with a bone!
Sinbad Now don't talk stupid, who would do that?
Mustapha (*blinking a lot*) Don't know.

Tinbad and Mrs Sinbad enter

Tinbad (*looking round; scared*) This is the sort of place where you meet gorillas and chimps . . .
Mrs Sinbad Then we'll be all right for a nice cup of P.G. Tips!
Sinbad (*impatiently*) Listen, you three! The Princess and my Talida are being dragged off to the Shrine of Love, and we've got to save them!
Mustapha You think we'll be all right? Isn't this the Jungle of Man-Eating Plants?
Tinbad (*reacting*) Man-Eating Plants? I'm frightened, I'm frightened!
Audience Kismet!
Tinbad (*with a big smile and "thumbs-up"*) Thanks — I'm all right now!
Mustapha (*to Tinbad*) Anyone seen a Man-Eating Plant?
Tinbad I've seen a man eating fish and chips.
Mrs Sinbad I heard of a hyena that swallowed an Oxo cube. He made a laughing stock of himself. (*Much amused*) A laughing stock of himself!!!!

Everyone laughs

A loud sucking noise is heard from the offstage mike and all stop laughing

Sinbad What was that?
Mustapha Sounds like Esther Rantzen cleaning her teeth.

The same squelchy sound is heard again

Sinbad Listen! We'd better be on guard.
Tinbad (*to the Audience*) If you see anything, will you shout out?
Mrs Sinbad Just shout out "It's him! It's him!" Zim! That's it! Just shout out ZIM!

A grotesque Plant enters, glides and wobbles across the stage and exits

Audience ZIM!
Tinbad Was that it?
Audience Yes! ZIM!
Tinbad You mean *here*? *Now*?
Audience Yes!
Mustapha Oh, I don't think so — I didn't see anything, did you, Mrs S?
Mrs Sinbad I felt a slight breeze round the bloomers . . .
Mustapha Well, we can look.

They all look round

Mustapha Nothing there.

Act II, Scene 3   47

Tinbad Tell us what to do, Sinbad.
Sinbad Well, when we reach the Shrine I want you to —
The Plant enters again, crosses the stage and exits
Audience ZIM!
All (*ad libbing*) Which side? That side? You sure? (*etc.*)
Mrs Sinbad If we don't want to be scared out of our yashmaks, I think we ought to sing. Anyone know a song about the jungle?
Tinbad (*singing unaccompanied*) "Jungle Bells, jungle bells".
All Lovely! We'll sing that!

They stand in a row and sing, unaccompanied, a parody of "Jingle Bells" —
Song 15

The Plant enters and scares off in turn Mustapha, Sinbad, Tinbad. Each suddenly sees the Plant and reacts with various versions of comedy terror, and runs off

Mrs Sinbad remains and the Plant moves beside her

Mrs Sinbad Oh, Tinbad, I am glad you're beside me to keep me company. Here, hold my hand 'cos I'm frightened. That's it dear. Tinbad, your nails need cutting! I can feel every finger nail! There are two, three, four, five, six (*slowing down*) seven . . . eight . . . nine . . .

It dawns on her — she looks at the Plant — screams loudly and it chases her offstage to loud vaudeville music accompaniment

Black-out

SCENE 3

The Shrine of Love and the Waters of Eternal Happiness

Hawaiian music is heard. The Slaves of the Shrine are in a tableau by the font and, moving slowly downstage as she speaks, is Bludruncolda, a beautiful but evil Egyptian/Druid Priestess

Bludruncolda I am Bludruncolda, the High Priestess of the Shrine of Love. (*She points to the font*) There is the magic water and once you have drunk from it, the next person you see, you will fall in love with for ever and for ever. I am the High Priestess and I have spoken.

She waves her Ceremonial Wand and all sing

Song 16

There is some ceremony with the goblets during the song and sometimes a solo by the Priestess or a Slave is introduced

After the Production Number, Sinistro and Crunchbones enter and both gaze round happily

Sinistro The Magical Waters! The Mystical Shrine!
The Princess Pearl will soon be mine!
Crunchbones Da Mystical Shrine! Da Magical Water!
Soon ma girl will do as she oughter!
Bludruncolda (*pleased, rubbing her hands together*) Greetings, Witchdoctor! We're three wicked and evil people together—what can I do for you gentlemen?
Sinistro We each love a girl—but the girls don't love us.
Bludruncolda The same old story. (*She calls*) Ashtak! Kalifah!

Two Slaves step forward

Take these two gentlemen, and prepare them for the ceremony!
Two Slaves (*together*) You command and we obey.

They exit with Crunchbones, the other Slaves following

Bludruncolda (*calling after them*) Gentlemen, soon the magical waters will turn your dreams into reality.
Sinistro (*to the Audience*) Everything's working out *beautifully*. Ha, ha, ha, ha!

He exits, following the others

Sinbad, Mrs Sinbad, Tinbad and Mustapha enter

Mustapha (*looking round*) What a nice sauna! It reminds of the (*local*) Baths!
Mrs Sinbad I went there once—one minute it was full, the next minute it was empty.
Mustapha Why, what happened?
Mrs Sinbad Cyril Smith jumped in.
Tinbad (*happily noticing the Priestess*) Ah! A lady of the female sex!
Bludruncolda I am the High Priestess. My name is Bludruncolda. What do you want, O insignificant one?
Tinbad (*to the Audience*) It's Dracula's mother! I'm frightened! I'm frightened!
Audience Kismet!
Tinbad ("*thumbs-up*") Thanks—I'm better now!
Bludruncolda What can I do for you people?
Sinbad We want to find our friends and then get back home and relax.
Mustapha Put our feet up and watch the telly.
Bludruncolda (*mystified*) Telly? What is Telly?
Mrs Sinbad *Television*, dear. (*To the Audience*) We've got a right one here.
Bludruncolda "Telly sishon?"
Tinbad (*to Mrs Sinbad*) She's potty. (*To the Priestess*) *Television*.
Sinbad (*also explaining*) We want to get back home and watch *television*.
Bludruncolda (*blankly; shaking her head*) I'm sorry …
Mrs Sinbad Don't you have television in Nirvana?
Bludruncolda No. What *is* television?
Tinbad You know, what you switch on. (*He mimes it*) Then you watch all the programmes.

Act II, Scene 3

Bludruncolda What is "programmes"? (*With sudden fury*) If you are trying to ridicule the High Priestess, you shall die.
Mustapha Oh no, not to die — tomorrow perhaps!
Bludruncolda You shall die! You shall die!
Mrs Sinbad (*aside to others*) We'd better show her the programmes!
Bludruncolda You are enemies of the Witchdoctor! You shall die!
Sinbad (*with great charm*) Oh, great Priestess, as you seem interested, may we have the pleasure of showing you some programmes?
Bludruncolda (*mollified*) It is true. I *am* interested. Show me.
Tinbad (*to the others*) We'd better keep on the right side of her!
Mustapha And keep her mind off other things!

They all look relieved as she sits on a downstage stool looking upstage

Mrs Sinbad (*to the others*) You go and get organized.

Mustapha, Tinbad and Sinbad exit

(*to the Priestess*) We just love television back home in Constantinople, and here are some of the programmes! I hope I remember them. (*To the Audience*) Here, if we get a bit muddled you'll help, won't you?

Mrs Sinbad runs offstage

Tinbad enters with a white cricket cap and a cricket bat. He mimes playing cricket

From one side Mrs Sinbad pops on with a notice saying "ZONK" and Sinbad from the other side with a notice saying "BIFF"

Bludruncolda What "programme" is that?
All three *Batman*!

All three exit
Mustapha enters quickly with a box of matches and strikes one

Bludruncolda What's that?
Mustapha *Match of the Day.*

Tinbad exits

NOTE: Audience involvement must happen, and can be included anywhere in this routine. Also, the Slaves of the Shrine can be involved if required — Mrs Sinbad would ask them to join in and assist her

Mrs Sinbad enters doing a hula-hula dance, holding up one hand showing all five fingers, and she says "Oh!"

Bludruncolda Please?
Mrs Sinbad *Hawaii-Five-O.*

Mrs Sinbad exits
Mustapha enters the other side with a large bit of cardboard and "Peter" printed in blue letters on it

Bludruncolda What programme?

Mustapha Blue Peter ... (*to the Audience*) Easy, isn't it?

Mustapha exits

Tinbad and Sinbad both rush in with a mallet in one hand and an L.P. in the other. They hit the L.P.s with the mallets

Bludruncolda What's that?
Tinbad ⎫
Sinbad ⎭ (*together*) ⎰ The Record Breakers.

Tinbad and Sinbad exit

Mrs Sinbad enters the other side with two local road signs at angles on a stick

Bludruncolda What programme please?
Mrs Sinbad *Crossroads*!

Mrs Sinbad exits

Mustapha enters, wearing a boxing glove

Tinbad comes on and Mustapha knocks him out

Bludruncolda And that?
Mustapha *It's a Knockout*!
Tinbad It very nearly was an' all ... I'll have a talk with you after the show ... very nearly killed me he did!

Tinbad and Mustapha exit

Mrs Sinbad enters with a fan and handkerchief. She fans herself and presses the handkerchief to her forehead

Bludruncolda What programme please?
Mrs Sinbad *It Ain't 'Arf Hot, Mum*.

Mrs Sinbad exits

Sinbad returns, blowing a steel whistle

Sinbad I'm testing ... (*He blows the whistle again*) I'm testing!
Bludruncolda And that is?
Sinbad *The Old Grey Whistle Test*.

Sinbad exits

Mrs Sinbad runs in, kneels down and Tinbad enters holding a crown. He holds it up over her head and slowly lowers it ceremoniously onto her head

Bludruncolda What is that programme?
Audience *Coronation Street*.
Tinbad Correct!

Tinbad and Mrs Sinbad exit

Mustapha runs in, stands centre stage but with knees bent and now mimes walking upstairs by gradually straightening his knees as he walks. He turns round and mimes walking downstairs

Act II, Scene 3

Bludruncolda And that is?
Mustapha (*with the Audience*) *Upstairs, Downstairs*!

Mrs Sinbad, Tinbad and Sinbad run in and join Mustapha in a group

With choreographed arm movements, to vaudeville chords, they all call out

The Four   It's colossal!
It's tremendous!
It's gigantic!
It's stupendous!
It's the greatest living wizard of the age —
It's Television — The greatest living wizard of the age!

The Four exit, waving

Bludruncolda, who has been enjoying herself, exits the opposite side

Mrs Sinbad and Tinbad enter patting their foreheads and fanning themselves

Mrs Sinbad Oh, I'm hot after that — I'm having one of my hot flushes.
Tinbad (*pointing to the font*) Well, there's some water.
Mrs Sinbad Don't touch it, it may be bad!
Tinbad Oh, I shouldn't think so.
Mrs Sinbad (*slapping his hand*) I said *don't touch it*, it wants boiling first!
Tinbad Well, I'm boiling so I'm going to take it and you can shut your trap.
Mrs Sinbad I wouldn't dream of drinking it. (*She takes goblet; shouting*) And you are a pain in the neck!
Tinbad Well, you're a cold in the head!
Mrs Sinbad You're the toothache!
Tinbad You're the mumps! (*To the Audience*) Shall I drink it? Shall I?
Audience No ... Yes ...! (*etc.*)
Tinbad Well, I'm going to give it a whirl.
(*Reciting*)   Round the teeth and round the gums
Look out tummy, here it comes!

He prepares to drink while Mrs Sinbad addresses the Audience

Mrs Sinbad Shall I gobble some of the water?
Audience No!
Mrs Sinbad (*not hearing*) Shall I gobble it out of this goblet?
Audience No!
Mrs Sinbad (*to the Audience*) Cheers!

Both Tinbad and Mrs Sinbad drink. At once we hear "Love Is A Many Splendoured Thing", or the Tchaikovsky "Romeo and Juliet" music, played double forte and instantly Tinbad and Mrs Sinbad register comedy romantic infatuation

  Oh, Knight in shining armour!
Tinbad Oh, my little herbaceous border!
Mrs Sinbad (*drinking again*) Oh, it's better than Ribena!
Tinbad If you were a chocolate I'd eat you! Where did you get those lovely blue eyes?

Mrs Sinbad They came with the face.
Tinbad I'm going to make you the happiest woman in the world!
Mrs Sinbad He's full of Eastern Promise!
Tinbad Voulez-vous dancer avec moi?
Mrs Sinbad Oh, it's Charles Asnohair!

The music becomes the introduction and they sing and dance with much "Come Dancing" romance

Song 17

During their routine they call out:

Tinbad (*romantically*) This is like something from the Arabian Nights ...
Mrs Sinbad Yes—we're dancing sheik to sheik ...

The Slaves of the Shrine enter singing and dancing in a thirties waltz style, carrying long, narrow lengths of gauze. Mrs Sinbad and Tinbad part and go to the opposite sides of the stage where they get entangled with the dancers and the gauze, and the thirties romantic atmosphere goes haywire

PRODUCTION NUMBER

After bows and curtsies, Tinbad and Mrs Sinbad exit followed by the Slaves

At the other side, Sinistro enters with the struggling Princess and Crunchbones enters with the struggling Talida. Bludruncolda enters from elsewhere and greets them

Bludruncolda And who are these two little dears?
Sinistro This is the girl I wish to marry, and that is the girl *he* wishes to marry.
Talida I'll never marry the Witchdoctor!
Bludruncolda (*evilly*) It's not for you to decide, my dear.
Princess Leave us alone! (*Aside to Talida, pointing offstage*) We must escape!
Talida Yes.

The two girls break free and start to exit

Bludruncolda (*waving her arms quickly at them*) NIRVANA!

The Princess and Talida become statues under her magic spell

Two Slaves enter near them and grab them

Slaves of the Shrine! (*She points*) Beside the Font of Eternal Happiness you will find there are ropes for those that disobey.

The Slaves take the two now placid girls and tie ropes round their wrists

(*to Sinistro and Crunchbones*) Now they are in your power. (*To the girls*) Foolish ones, your time has come.

Sinbad enters heroically

Sinbad It hasn't! I'm here to rescue Talida and the Princess! I'm not afraid of you! I may be only Sinbad the Sailor but—

Act II, Scene 3   53

> During his speech all the Slaves of the Shrine enter and two of them grab Sinbad

Bludruncolda (*evilly*) Silence, oh Sinbad the Sailor. You will stay *there* and watch the ceremony. Gentlemen, take the goblets of water.

> Sinistro and Crunchbones take the goblets

The maiden of your choice cannot resist my magic and will now become your wife. (*To Sinbad*) Nothing can save your friends now, Sinbad the Sailor. (*To Sinistro and Crunchbones*) Force the girls to drink, go on, force them! Force them! Force them!

> Dramatic music is heard and there is a struggle near the Font as the two girls are held still by the Slaves, their faces in profile. Sinistro and Crunchbones put the goblets to the girls' mouths

(*gloating; over the dramatic music*) So you love the Caliph of Constantinople and you love Sinbad the Sailor. But not any more! Not when the Waters of Eternity have been poured down your beautiful throats!

Sinistro
Crunchbones } (*together*) { One ... two ...

Old Man (*off*) STOP!

> The dramatic music stops dead, and the Old Man of the Sea enters

All on stage react with surprise and fear

Bludruncolda (*gasping*) The Old Man of the Sea! (*She bows to him*)

The Old Man turns first to Sinbad, then to Crunchbones

Old Man   Brave young Sinbad the Sailor
                     You were good and spared my life!
                     So *you*, you nasty reptile
                     You shall not take her to wife!

He then turns to Sinistro

                     And you, dragging this girl around
                     Just like she were cattle
                     Behold—The Sword of Solomon
                     Which never lost a battle!

From behind him he holds up a sword and hands it to Sinbad

Bludruncolda takes a sword from a Slave and hands it to Sinistro

Bludruncolda   Now my friend let the duel begin
                     May wickedness, evil and cruelty win!

Dramatic music starts, the two girls get free from their ropes

Talida No, Sinbad, he will kill you!
Princess Be careful, Sinbad!
Crunchbones Mister Sinistro, sir, you *annihilate* him!

The duel begins with the two combatants circling each other

Sinbad All right then, Sinistro, now let's see who's the victor!
Sinistro I have the sword of the Priestess!
Sinbad I have the Sword of Solomon—so put that bread knife away!

Everyone cheers Sinbad's words

Sinistro I have evil on my side!
Sinbad I have goodness—that means I shall win!
Sinistro Never, you puny little sailor.
Bludruncolda Success to you, O Sinistro, and may villainy be victorious!

The duel commences, accompanied by "fight" music

Princess (*shouting*) May Allah grant that Sinbad may win!
Talida Sinbad, you must win!
Old Man Come on, me boy, please the Old Man of the Sea!
Others (*chanting the letters*) S—I—N—B—A—D ... Sinbad!

Sinbad wins when Sinistro trips and falls and Sinbad points his sword at his throat

Crunchbones Disaster! Calamity! Boombah! (*He shakes his head, depressed*)
Sinbad (*to the Audience*) What shall I do with him?
Audience Kill him!
Sinbad (*laughing*) Why you bloodthirsty lot! I've got a better idea! (*To the Priestess*) I think you two were made for each other. (*To the Audience and to all those on stage*) Don't you agree?
Slaves Yes!
Sinistro (*with great drama*) Infamy! Infamy! You've all got it in-for-me!
Bludruncolda (*ice-cold; cruelly*) I am willing. (*She goes to Sinistro and attempts a seductive smile*)
Sinistro (*mournfully to the Audience with a sob*) Everything's turned out beautifully ... oh ... oh ... oh ...
Old Man Drink, both of you, drink!

Sinistro and the Priestess drink and then gaze enraptured at each other

Sinistro Sheila Easton!
Bludruncolda Mick Jagger!
Sinbad And you, you wicked old Witchdoctor, you shall drink and the first maiden of the shrine you shall see, you shall marry.
Crunchbones (*pleased*) Me very happy! Me thank you very much for kindness! Ho, ho, ho!

He takes a goblet, drinks and waits, delighted

A slave girl enters with blacked-out teeth and red nose and thick frames to her glasses

Slave Girl Hullo, sexy!
Crunchbones (*turning round*) Hullo and—(*he groans*)—Oh no, no!

But there is a "ting" from percussion and they fall in love. The Princess takes two goblets and hands them to Talida and Sinbad as all form a tableau

Act II, Scene 3

Princess At last, no more worry and no more grief!
Soon I'll be home and I'll marry the Caliph!

Sinbad and Talida drink to each other

Sinbad May Allah look down on us and bless
Talida As we drink the Waters of Happiness!

As Sinbad and Talida gaze at each other all cheer then reprise the last eight bars of Song 6

Song 6 (reprise)

Mustapha has also fallen for a slave girl, and Mrs Sinbad and Tinbad have re-entered, so the five couples hold hands and gaze rapturously at each other as they sing

Black-out

Scene 4

On board Sinbad's ship returning home

During the Black-out, Tinbad and Sinistro step downstage and at once lights come up on them, the tabs closing behind them

Sinistro *(fiercely)* You! I want you to help me!
Tinbad *(surprised)* Me help *you*?
Sinistro I'm getting married to the High Priestess and I'm trapped! It'll be like living with a battleship! I'm terrified of her! What can I do?
Tinbad Oh my friends will help you there. Whenever you're scared just say "I'm frightened, I'm frightened" and they'll cheer you up.
Sinistro Really?
Tinbad *(nodding)* It works like a dream.

The High Priestess enters

Bludruncolda Ah, there you are, my little dumpling. Who is Bludruncolda's little baby, then? *(Returning to her former manner)* Sinistro, why aren't you at home doing the washing up?
Tinbad Go on!
Sinistro *(to the Audience)* I'm frightened, I'm frightened!
Audience Kismet!
Sinistro *("thumbs-up" to the Audience)* Thanks — I'm better now! *(Sternly to Bludruncolda)* You're my wife now so you'll do as you're told. We're going down to the disco.
Bludruncolda *(meekly)* Yes, dear. *(Jazzing it up suddenly; wildly out of character)* Play me some Pink Floyd — Hot Gossip — Blondie — Barry Manilow!
Sinistro *(to the Audience, delighted)* What a little raver!

They exit arm in arm to a few bars of rock

Tinbad Wasn't that nice? Well we're all getting married and I think that calls for a celebration. So now we're going back home on Sinbad's ship, why don't we sing about *another* ship. I'm afraid you won't know the song, it's called *Yellow Submarine* (*or other choice*) does anyone know it?
Audience Yes!
Tinbad All right, don't shout, I'm not blind! *Yellow Submarine* . . . I once met an Irishman that went to sleep in a submarine — with the windows open. (*Calling offstage*) Anybody got the words of "*Yellow Submarine*"?

Coca and Cola enter with a cut-out of a yellow submarine with the words on it, but they are holding it upside down

Tinbad By Allah, it's you two again! What have you done wrong this time?
Coca
Cola } (*together, giggling*) { Nothing.
Tinbad It's upside down.
Coca What is? (*She sees it*) Aren't we stupid?
Cola Sorry!

They turn it the right way up as Tinbad addresses the Audience

Tinbad Now each time you get to the words "yellow submarine", put up the periscope like this.

He demonstrates by stretching his arm up and swivelling his hand, then he sings, joined by Coca and Cola

Song 18

The Audience sings with him and does the "up periscope" business at the various places in the song when encouraged by him.

After one chorus, Mrs Sinbad enters in outrageous gear — her finale dress underneath

Mrs Sinbad What on earth was all that noise about? I've never heard anything so terrible! You call that singing?
Tinbad (*to the Audience*) We were very good, weren't we?
Audience Yes!
Tinbad (*pointing*) Particularly *this* side, this side was a lot better than *that*.
Mrs Sinbad What cheek! (*To the other side*) You hear that? You're not going to stand for that, are you? No, so you can sit down and sing back. Come on! (*She conducts her side in the song with gestures*)

As she conducts her team so Tinbad and his group boo. Then when Tinbad and his group sing, Mrs Sinbad's group boo back

Our side was best — oh yes it was! (Oh, no it wasn't)

All sing the last chorus with periscope gestures

Tinbad and Mrs Sinbad exit, waving

There is a fanfare, the Wazir enters and bangs the floor with his stick

Act II, Scene 4

Wazir Pray silence for the Ruler of the Seventeen Mountains, the Caliph of Constantinople!

The Caliph enters in finale costume

Caliph (*to the Audience*) O good people, I invite you to the wedding! Sinbad has returned the Princess to me and so great is my delight that I have bestowed on him half my kingdom. (*He raises his arms*) So may Allah watch over you and may you now behold my wedding to the Princess—
Wazir And Sinbad's wedding—
Caliph And *Mrs* Sinbad's wedding—
Wazir And the Witchdoctor's wedding—
Caliph And the wicked Sinistro's wedding—
Wazir And Mustapha's wedding—
Caliph Yes, Allah has granted that *all* of us shall be wedded in
Wazir } (*together*) { The Palace of a Million Minarets!
Caliph

Fanfare as he and the Wazir exit separate sides, and the tabs open

Scene 5

Sinbad's wedding in the Palace of a Million Minarets in Constantinople

Finale walk down and the first to enter clap in time to the music of Song 3, and get the Audience to clap with the tempo

All take their bows and the last two are Sinbad and Talida who are greeted with a cheer from the cast. When all have lined up, they speak the finale couplets

Sinistro	Sinbad has travelled the Seven Seas!
Sinbad	From Egypt to Australia!
Mrs Sinbad	Oh, look he's gone down on his knees!
Tinbad	Let me offer you this Dahlia!
Mrs Sinbad	(*coyly*) Oh, you shouldn't ...

Tinbad kneels and offers a big artificial flower to her—she takes the top part with the flower itself but the stem stays in his hand (or the other way round!). All laugh and sing the last chorus, waving goodbyes

Final chorus

Curtain

FURNITURE AND PROPERTY LIST

(See also notes on Settings and Costumes which follow this list)

ACT I

SCENE 1 (and SCENE 2)

On stage: Basket with snake
Piece of plank (for SCENE 2)

Off stage: Two boards — one with **KIS** on it and the other with **MET** on it
Sedan chair with false back
Laundry rope with washing on it

Personal: **Sinistro:** large book with pictures of the Princess in it
Mrs Sinbad: coloured bag. *In it:* plastic toilet seat, bars of chocolate, packet of Tide. Hat with false fish. Crab/lobster on back of skirt
Wazir: stick of office
Galley girl: duster

SCENE 3

On stage: Statue

Off stage: Ropes (**Natives**)
Plastic bag with pheasant and £5 note (**Mrs Sinbad**)

Personal: **Crunchbones:** bones (used throughout)
Sinbad: sword
Mrs Sinbad: handbag

SCENE 4

Personal: **Sinistro:** jewel on chain
Mrs Sinbad: Handbag. *In it:* shears

SCENE 5

Off stage: Scimitar (**Sinbad**)

ACT II

SCENE 1

Set: Nest
Off stage: Baskets of fruit, etc. (**Islanders**)
Picnic basket. *In it:* three tablecloths with nylon lines attached, food as indicated, toilet rolls, transistor radio, kettle, French loaf, etc. (**Mrs Sinbad** and **Tinbad**)

Scene 2

No props required

Scene 3

On stage: Goblets by font
Stool

Personal: **Bludruncolda:** wand

Off stage: Two notices (ZAK and BIFF) (**Mrs Sinbad** and **Sinbad**)
Match (**Tinbad**)
Cricket cap and bat (**Tinbad**)
Card with PETER in blue (**Mustapha**)
Two LPs (**Tinbad** and **Sinbad**)
Two mallets (**Tinbad** and **Sinbad**)
Two roadsigns (**Mrs Sinbad**)
Boxing gloves (**Mustapha**)
Fan, handkerchief (**Mrs Sinbad**)
Whistle (**Sinbad**)
Crown (**Tinbad**)
Sword (**Old Man**)
Sword (**Slave**)

Scene 4

Off stage: Cut-out of yellow submarine (or alternative) with words of song on it

Scene 5

Off stage: Flower (**Tinbad**)

LIGHTING PLOT

External settings throughout

ACT I, Scene 1 and Scene 2

To open: Bright sunshine

Cue 1	After production number of Song 2 *Lights darken; spot on Sinistro*	(Page 4)
Cue 2	**Sinbad** joins **Sinistro** *Lights revert to normal*	(Page 5)
Cue 3	**Sinistro** creates a spell *Lights fade down*	(Page 6)
Cue 4	**Sinistro** "... of his dreams to him." *Half light behind gauze*	(Page 6)
Cue 5	**Sinbad:** "... fabulous sorcerer all right." *Fade light on gauze. Back to previous level*	(Page 6)
Cue 6	**Sinistro** casts a spell *Darken lighting. Lightning*	(Page 11)
Cue 7	**Sinistro:** "... that is frightening." *Cease lightning*	(Page 11)
Cue 8	**Sinistro** laughs evilly *Lightning. Dramatic lighting*	(Page 11)
Cue 9	**Sinistro** exits with **Princess** *Revert to normal lighting*	(Page 11)
Cue 10	As all exit after Song 4 *Black-out*	(Page 16)

ACT I, Scene 3

To open: Weird lighting, perhaps strobe

Cue 11	**Sinistro:** "... who's in command." *Lights dim. Stone idol's eyes light up*	(Page 19)
Cue 12	**Witchdoctor** collects bones *Lights revert to normal*	(Page 20)
Cue 13	**Tinbad, Mrs Sinbad** and **Mustapha** chase off *Black-out*	(Page 25)

Sinbad The Sailor

ACT I, SCENE 4

To open: Outdoor lighting

Cue 14	**Sinistro** exits to Grotto *Lights darken. Green spot on Old Man*	(Page 26)
Cue 15	**Sinbad** and **Talida** enter *Revert to normal*	(Page 27)

ACT I, SCENE 5(a)

To open: Weird, spooky lighting

ACT I, SCENE 5(b)

To open: Bright, dazzling light

ACT II, SCENE 1

To open: Outdoor lighting

Cue 16	Music 14 becomes thunderously loud *Strobe effect*	(Page 43)
Cue 17	**Islanders** cry out in terror *Black-out*	(Page 43)

ACT II, SCENE 2

To open: Dim lighting

Cue 18	**Plant** chases **Mrs Sinbad** off *Black-out*	(Page 47)

ACT II, SCENE 3

To open: Outdoor lighting

Cue 19	At end of Song 6 (reprise) *Black-out*	(Page 55)

ACT II, SCENE 4

To open: Outdoor lighting

No cues

ACT II, SCENE 5

To open: Outdoor lighting

No cues

EFFECTS PLOT

ACT I

Cue 1	**Mrs Sinbad** throws fish into wings *Splash*	(Page 7)
Cue 2	**Mrs Sinbad:** "I married him." *Oriental fanfare*	(Page 8)
Cue 3	**Mrs Sinbad** and **Sinbad** exit *Fanfare*	(Page 8)
Cue 4	**Mustapha:** "That'll be enough." *Fanfare*	(Page 9)
Cue 5	**Sinistro** casts a spell *Thunder*	(Page 11)
Cue 6	**Sinistro:** "... that is frightening." *Cease thunder*	(Page 11)
Cue 7	**Sinistro** laughs cruelly *Thunder*	(Page 11)
Cue 8	**Caliph:** "Come back, you villain!" *Flash in footlights*	(Page 11)
Cue 9	In Black-out after Scene 2 *Drum beats, cannibal cries*	(Page 16)
Cue 10	**Sinistro:** "... who's in command." *Thunder*	(Page 19)
Cue 11	As stage darkens after Sinistro's exit *Mysterious music*	(Page 26)
Cue 12	**Old Man of the Sea:** "... Waters of Paradise!" *Fanfare*	(Page 33)
Cue 13	**Old Man of the Sea:** "... so I must obey!" *Fanfare*	(Page 33)

ACT II

Cue 14	As food, etc. whizzes off stage *Swanee whistle*	(Pages 37–38)
Cue 15	**Sinbad:** "What's that?" *Wind effect*	(Page 42)
Cue 16	To open Scene 2 *Bird song, jungle effects*	(Page 43)

Sinbad The Sailor 63

Cue 17	**Mrs Sinbad:** "... laughing stock of himself." *Fierce sucking noise*	(Page 46)
Cue 18	**Mustapha:** "... cleaning her teeth." *Squelching sound*	(Page 46)
Cue 19	As **Wazir** enters *Fanfare*	(Page 56)
Cue 20	As **Wazir** and **Caliph** exit *Fanfare*	(Page 57)

SCENERY AND COSTUME SUGGESTIONS

This pantomime has been presented in large professional theatres and yet it also works well with a simple production and a small stage. If you are planning a spectacular production—and the subject does lend itself to spectacle—you will have your own plans. For a small production these notes will be of help:

Setting
Every scene is an exterior so the palm tree wings can be permanent. A cyclorama upstage suits this outdoor subject and into this Permanent Set goes the following, none of which is complicated:

ACT ONE
For **Scene One** (in Constantinople) put cut-outs of oriental onion-domed buildings in front of the permanent palm tree wings. Upstage is a highly ornamental Eastern galleon or "dhow" which isn't practical so can be a backcloth. Part of it is painted gauze through which the magic vision of the principal girl will be seen later. The Beggar's snake rises by means of a nylon wire attached to the end of the flute and also to the snake in the basket. As the flute is raised, so the snake rises, and as the flute is moved about so the snake seems to sway. **Scene Two** is tabs, or a frontcloth of the deck of Sinbad's ship. In Arabian Nights illustrations, the sails and woodwork are brown and orange. **Scene Three** has the permanent palm tree wings, the cyclorama to represent the sea and seashore, and the Easter Island-style stone god statue that looks like a massive and ugly totem pole about 8 feet high and 3 feet wide. If it is at centre stage, unseen nylon lines, when pulled, cause the totem to break in two, as though by magic. If the statue is touching the one wing, this falling apart of the statue is easily manipulated from offstage. **Scene Four** (outside the Grotto) is tabs or a frontcloth of dull pink coral with seaweed and an oddly shaped entrance to the Grotto. **Scene Five** (Grotto interior) is dim and spooky with weird stalactites which are cut-outs in front of the palm tree wings. Stalactite cut-outs should also hide the cyclorama for the moment. Six crates have dull pink stalagmite cut-outs nailed on to their fronts. On these crates stand some of the Chorus as the sinister-looking "Living Statues"—it is called a "dark horror scene" which transforms by either flying the gloomy pink coral backcloth or by pulling off into the wings the large stalactite and stalagmite cut-outs, thus revealing a Great Gateway through which can be seen the cyclorama. Pea lights or larger electric bulbs on the Gates, which don't have to open, help the "dazzle" for this Interval Curtain moment.

ACT TWO

Scene One is the same as Act I, Scene Three but instead of the totem statue we have a big (8 feet long by 4 feet high) cut-out of a nest with entwined branches and twigs and a couple of huge eggs in it — all painted on the cut-out. If a green ravine/valley backcloth was used behind the Gates at the end of Act I, it is still in position as we are now in the valley proper. In front of the palm tree wings there are cut-outs of green rocks with blobs of crunched-up green metal foil wrapping paper to represent emeralds. Some have a small green light in them. **Scene Two** is tabs or a frontcloth of a mysterious jungle with snakes wrapped round the trees. **Scene Three** is The Shrine. Cut-outs of orientally-shaped obelisks are in front of each palm tree wing and upstage centre is The Shrine with its pagoda roof. This is a large creeper-covered font that doesn't look like a pretty wishing well but is strange and oriental. On the floor or on the rim of the great Font are goblets. **Scene Four** is the songsheet. **Scene Five** is the Finale and the two cut-outs of buildings used in Act I, Scene One are reversed, showing their backs painted silver or gold with Arabian filigree work for the Finale wings. Upstage centre, in front of the cyclorama, is a Moorish arch or a cut-out of a domed building with many minarets that is somewhat like the Taj Mahal.

Costumes
Due to the story, the Principals have no costume changes though **Mrs Sinbad**'s Arabian costume should change due to the traditions of pantomime Dame. **Tinbad** wears a large comedy turban and a horizontally striped jersey and baggy Arabian trousers. **Sinistro** is in dark green or purple with signs of the Zodiac. **Talida** is Hawaiian style. **Crunchbones**, the Witchdoctor, wears over the top part of his face a mask that includes his nose so that a white tusk appears to have been pushed through his nose. He wears a terrifying headdress of feathers and a skull or animal's head, with a leopard skin over his body. **Sinbad** wears a bright blue turban and a "principal boy sailor" style coat or tunic. The **Old Man of the Sea** is bent-backed, has much white hair and beard; his costume is seaweedy and scraggy — something like a senile King Neptune. Blacked-out teeth and claw-like hands add to his weird appearance. **Bludruncolda** wears Greek Tragedy-style robes, carries a large ornamental staff of office or crook, and can have a skull-cap with "widow's peak" over her forehead. **Coca** and **Cola** look attractive in their slave girl/harem costumes, **Mustapha** is comedy Eastern and **El Hump**, the Camel, is a yellow-brown pantomime horse skin with a polystyrene and canvas hump. **The Man-Eating Plant** has the human head and face hidden by a group of canvas leaves or petals upwards from the neck, a green smeared gown to the floor and his or her hands are green gloves with extremely long fingers, the arms continually sway and wave about, and the fingers viciously snap about.

Chorus. The Citizens of Constantinople are as seen in Arabian Nights illustrated books — "Arab Sheikh tarboosh" headdresses, turbans with big earrings attached, fezes, brightly coloured waistcoats, harem-style trousers. The Natives of Nirvana are Hawaiian style, the Living Statues are Hawaiian with a great deal of grey and black sinister-looking scrim and gauze draped over them. The Exotic Birds are the juveniles in leotards, with masks and wings. The Slaves of the Shrine have saris over their Hawaiian costumes or are in Ancient Greek-style robes/gowns. If the above "costume additions" are worn over the Hawaiian costumes the Chorus (except for Scene One in Constantinople) can wear the same costume throughout.

The Giant Roc Bird's Arrival
This is the most famous moment in all the voyages of Sinbad. A projection of it, such as a slide showing the bird, was used in a professional production but doesn't work well nor does someone entering dressed as the Roc Bird. These two ideas make for an anti-climax and I suggest one of the following ideas:

The Roc Bird is not a human in a costume but is Scenery and is as impressive as possible. It can be a big cut-out that rises up from behind the Giant Bird's Nest, rather as the Beanstalk in *Jack* is sometimes pulled upwards by nylon lines. This way we would see its head first, but in the following other ways, we would see the feet first as the Bird would appear downwards. A good idea is a large cut-out of canvas and hardboard flown in, rather as the silver bells are flown in from the flies in *Dick Whittington*. So big claws would appear first. It can be that a nylon wire pulls it downward from above and it is a sort of Venetian blind that unrolls in the shape of the legs and body of the bird. It can be a very large cut-out of hardboard that is pushed on from the wings on a trolley, preferably behind the groundrow. I have seen it as a very large prop "flying" towards the stage from the back of the audience on a wire.

Whichever way is chosen, the scale should be *massive* and its arrival is accompanied by dramatic music and the cawing sound effects and the flickering lights. This prevents the audience from seeing a brightly-lit "Bird" which would spoil the illusion. The cast's terrified reaction further helps to tell our story.

John Morley

MADE AND PRINTED IN GREAT BRITAIN BY
LATIMER TREND & COMPANY LTD PLYMOUTH
MADE IN ENGLAND